"Fran Costigan's creations are delectable, rich tasting and gorgeous. Everyone lucky enough to t $2.50 her treats is shocked to discover what they do not contain – dairy-eggs-butter and refined sweeteners! Fran's commitment to using organic, seasonal ingredients and her support of local growers is very strong, you can taste the freshness – and the berries and the lemon and the chocolate...."

> -Jeanette Maier & Adam Ruderman
> Co-Owners, Herban Kitchen,
> New York City, New York

"It's a good thing Fran has written this very real book. Now, anyone who wants uncompromising desserts can have them both ways--satisfyingly yummy and consciously healthy."

> -Leslie McEachern
> Owner, Angelica Kitchen,
> New York City, New York

"The search is over for great non-dairy desserts! Perfect cakes, cookies and other delicious baked goods are a guarantee when you use Fran Costigan's recipes. The Candle Café acknowledges Fran and especially her decadent 'Chocolate Cake To Live For.' For goodness sake, we love her and her cakes."

> -Joy Pierson, Nutritionist and Bart Potenza
> Co-owners The Candle Café
> New York City, New York

"I just indulged in yet another DELICIOUS piece of Fran's famous chocolate cake, complete with chocolate frosting, chocolate shavings and her vanilla frozen dessert. YUM! Fran, you nailed that frosting recipe. It is amazing and really hard to believe it contains so little fat. It will become my staple frosting recipe. To give people healthy, sustainable (health-wise, planet-wise, animal-wise) recipes is a wonderful gift. Thanks for sharing your talents with the world."

> -John D. Borders, JD
> Chair, Board of Directors, Earthsave International

"You know those days when you just need a chocolate fix? There is only one remedy and for me it is Fran Costigan's Chocolate Cake. I still can't believe there is no butter, no eggs, no sugar. Now lucky us, when we can't get to Fran, we can make one of her cakes or cookies, pies or puddings. Thanks Fran."

> -Elinor Tatum
> Publisher and Editor, The Amsterdam News

"Desserts are my priority and I won't settle for less than scrumptious! But I am committed to eating healthfully and avoid processed foods. It is fun for me to order a platter of cookies or a special cake from you, and serve them to customers and guests. Then, when they are saying yummy (and they always do), let them know the secret – healthy' sweets. Fran, you are one of the greatest pastry chefs in the world and an inspiration. I honor your work and thank you for creating reliable recipes for incredible desserts and treats – all with the best, healthful ingredients."

> -Gigi Pardo-Lord
> Sales manager

Cover design by Edgard Moscatelli, T Design, New York City, NY

Printed in the United States of America

Photograph of author by M. David Leeds, New York City, NY

Jewelry courtesy Aaro Studio, New York City, New York

Published by Good Cakes Productions
Good Cakes Publications
295 Greenwich Street / PMB-115
NYC, NY 10007-1049

Distributed by The Book Publishing Company
        P. O. Box 99
        Summertown, TN 38483
        800-695-2241

ISBN 0-9673108-0-6

Library of Congress Catalogue Card Number 99-073327

Great Good Desserts Naturally
Secrets of Sensational Sin-Free Sweets
Includes Index

Great Good Desserts

naturally!

Secrets of sensational sin-free sweets

Fran Costigan

This book is dedicated to Michael and Tracy,
the cookie monsters in my heart, and to all the kind-hearted
people who endeavor to honor the sweetness in all life.

Acknowledgements

Writing a cookbook is, for the most part, a solitary project and I certainly spent many hours alone in my kitchen and at my computer. But, when I began to list all the wonderful people who helped me throughout the process, I remembered that I was never really alone.

I must first acknowledge my students whose enthusiasm and good ideas make my work an on going pleasure. You asked for this book. A special thank you goes to Annemarie Colbin, author and Founding Director of the Natural Gourmet Institute of Food and Healing, for sparking and continuing my interest in whole foods. Whenever there is a question about new research, I know I can always count on Annemarie for her up to date, practical and prompt answers. Thank you Diane Carlson and Jenny Matthau, co-directors, and to the entire staff at the Natural Gourmet Institute of Food and Healing, for giving me the opportunity to teach and to continue to learn.

I have the very good luck to count among my colleagues, my good friends, Leslie McEachern, owner of Angelica Kitchen, Chef Ken Bergeron and Richard Pierce, the director of NYC's Whole Foods Project. I thank each of you for sharing a wealth of information and wonderful meals with me, and I know that your forthcoming books are sure to become classics. Jeanette Maier, chef-owner and Adam Ruderman, co-owner of Herban Kitchen, supplied me with maple syrup and more whenever I found my bottles empty at 11pm. I thank you both.

For encouragement, support and practical advice, I want to say thank you to my long-distance, well-published food writing friends, Jennifer Raymond, Bryanna Clark Grogin and Gail Davis. Vesanto Melina, R.D. is a lovely woman who has been an important source of information. And big thanks and hugs to my friends at the North American Vegetarian Society (NAVS) and Earthsave for excellent good works, great conferences and loads of fun. I owe a great debt to Kathryn Arnold for my first writing assignments and much encouragement.

Thank you Chef Shirley King, master cooking teacher, cookbook author and dear friend for your encouragement and feedback. Michael Romano, executive chef-partner of Union Square Cafe, thank you for generously sharing information, providing inspiration and urging me for years to write a guide to non-dairy baking. And Lorna Sass, I thank you for your practical advice and informative cookbooks. Having an e-mail question answered and having a laugh with Arch Corriher when Shirley, (Cookwise), Corriher was out of the country, amazed and delighted me. Thank you very much.

Special thanks to my colleague and new friend, Mimi Clark, owner of Veggie Gourmet Cooking Classes in Fairfax, VA, for her enthusiastic support, considerable knowledge and super sharp eyes.

Elaine Reader; you are indeed a fast and thorough reader with a great sense of humor; thank you. Thank you Leah Breier for always making time to answer a question. Cousin Sheila, your books inspire me and our talks nourish me.

Thanks to my mom, Shirley and Wini, my second mom, for introducing me to good food and to Dad, for eating cakes that melted on the way to Florida and liking them anyway. I wish to acknowledge the talented Leeds men: Peter, David and Phillip for love, support and good appetites. To Suzy, Philip, and Maddie: thank you for everything (but not for moving). To Lisa and Ron: my gratitude for your friendship, asking for tastes, keys to the office, working on the cover and weekends at the beach. Kiwon and Ronnie, your friendship means so much to me, what would I have done if you had not moved to Tribeca? Dear Mary and Fred, many thanks for good cheer, good music, interesting talk and the Fourth Estate, the best spot in Tribeca for a paper and a cup of something hot.

To help me make friends with my Mac and begin the design process, I thank Charlie Mendoza, the technical expert who explains the unexplainable in clear, plain English. I wish to acknowledge Sandi Schroeder for taking files and making an index. Sharon Mazel, a gifted editor who works at the speed of light, stepped in and brought me into the 90's. Thank you Sharon. Many thanks to my primary recipe testers, Gypsy, Mary, Doug, and Peter, readers; Mary, Rajesh, Jane and James and my friends and neighbors who gladly ate the cakes and cookies. I owe a special thank you to Elizabeth Woodbridge, my ace assistant, whose organizational skills and understanding of natural foods are a blessing. It has been a pleasure to work with her.

Edgard Moscatelli is a talented designer and perfectly wonderful person who kept his cool no matter what. Edgard, you are the best, and I am so glad to have had the opportunity to work with you.

All the people I've mentioned worked hard to make this book a reality, but if it not for my dear friend, Jimmy Nicholas, printer to the stars, I would still be saying, "the book is coming soon." Jimmy, as you have so many times over so many years, you said DO IT and did. Thank you is not enough.

Recipe List

FRUIT JELL-O

BLUEBERRY JELL

FRUIT SOUP & SALAD

SILKEN CASHEW CREAM

TROPICAL FRUIT MOUSSE

MY T GOOD CHOCOLATE PUDDING

CHOCOLATE SHERBET-SORBET

MAPLE GINGER, ALMOND

    & HAZELNUT CREAMS

LET THEM EAT BREAD PUDDING

TASTES LIKE IT COULD BE HARD SAUCE

CREAMY BROWN RICE & RAISIN PUDDING

MAPLE CIDER SAUCE

BASIC WHEAT-FREE COOKIE

ORANGE GINGER CRISPS

OATMEAL RAISIN COOKIES

HONEY-FREE SAVE THE BEES BAKLAVA

CAROB FUDGE BROWNIES

DOUBLE CHOCOLATE FUDGE BROWNIES

FRANKLY AMAZING LOW-FAT

    CHOCOLATE BROWNIE

A GOOD PAN OF CORNBREAD

PEANUT BUTTER PUFFED CEREAL TREATS

CRUNCHY CARAMEL POPCORN TREATS

GOOD GOURMET GORP

PEANUT BUTTER CHOCOLATE CANDY CUPS

THE VERSATILE VANILLA CAKE

BASIC TOFU CREAM FROSTING

TROPICAL FRUIT GATEAU

LEMON-LIME TOFU CREAM

LOVELY LIGHT LEMON CAKE

LUSCIOUS LEMONY TOFU CREAM

THE CHOCOLATE CAKE TO LIVE FOR

CHOCOLATE TOFU CREAM

ULTIMATE CHOCOLATE SAUCE

ULTIMATE CHOCOLATE FROSTING

Recipe List

LEMON GLAZED 24 KARAT CAKE

DREAMY LEMON CREAM

CAROB CAKE

CAROB ICING

BETTER BOSTON CREAM PIE

CUSTARD CREAM FILLING

CAROB GLAZE

UNCOFFEE CAKE

PEANUT BUTTER & JELLY POWER MUFFINS

MAPLE GLAZED CRANBERRIES

ORIGINAL FOOLPROOF FLAKY PIE DOUGH

NEWEST FOOLPROOF FLAKY PIE DOUGH

THIS IS NOT MY MOTHER'S PUMPKIN PIE

FREEFORM APPLESAUCE GALETTE

STRAWBERRY RHUBARB-APPLESAUCE TART

FRESH STRAWBERRY SAUCE

FANCY SUMMER FRUIT TARTS

THREE GLAZES FOR TARTS

RUSTIC 3 BERRY PIE

BERRY CRISP IN A COOKIE PIECRUST

CHOCOLATE GLAZED

STRAWBERRY SHORTCAKES

BLUEBERRY SLUMP

CRUMB TOPPING FOR COBBLERS & FRUIT PIES

BAKED APPLE BISCUIT TOPPED COBBLER

CREAMY STRAWBERRY-DATE FILLING

HINT OF LEMON CUSTARD SAUCE

ANNEMARIE'S APPLE JUICE KUZU PUDDING

HOT COCOA

NEW YORK EGGLESS CREAM

INSTANT AMAZAKE ICE CREAM

BAKED STUFFED APPLES

VANILLA BEAN N'ICE MILK

ANYTIME MEUSLI

NUTTY FROZEN BANANAS POPS

POACHED PEACHES (nectarines too)

Fran Costigan's

Great
Good
Desserts
naturally!

Secrets of sensational sin-free sweets

Contents

Chapter 1

Getting Started

Healthy Desserts 101

Because we can eat healthfully and have some fun too!

Introducing Great Good Desserts Naturally

I'm told my first words were 'More cake, please.'

I do not know if it is true, but mom did serve ice cream for breakfast. "It's milk," she would say. Food, sweets in particular, was important business in my family. We argued about brands of chocolate syrup (Uncle Harvey tolerated only one) and hoarded chocolate covered marshmallow cookies because they weren't available during summer. Eating enough (ice cream, cookies, brownies) meant the container was empty, but our sweets frenzy went hand in hand with constant dieting. At the end of any self-imposed dessert deprivation, we ate too many cookies again, and the cycle continued.

Early memories stayed with me and have certainly informed my journey, from a sweets-obsessed cookie monster, to a pastry chef–instructor. I specialize in developing and teaching recipes for *great tasting-good for you, non-dairy, refined sugar-free desserts and other treats.* Natural ingredients are used exclusively.

Today I enjoy reasonable amounts of healthful sweets, but the big kid who was dying for a cookie had to learn a thing or two first. My first job after culinary school was pastry cook in a gourmet take-out food shop on the Upper East Side of Manhattan. I made muffins, cookies, puddings, pies, cakes, popovers and a daily special 4 days a week. My desserts were popular and I loved the work, but I did not feel well most of the time. I ate (milk) chocolate for breakfast and grabbed cookies instead of lunch. My energy fluctuated wildly as did my mood. I left my job after six months wondering why I did not have the stamina to do the work I absolutely adored. I decided to take some time off.

I began to travel with my former husband, Peter and the rock n' roll band he managed. One day, wanting to break the monotony of watching a video shoot, I wandered into a bookstore looking for some easy summer reading. I chose instead several books on healthful diet, including the seminal volume, *Food and Healing* by Annemarie Colbin. Ms. Colbin writes that

while no one diet is right for everyone, the SAD (Standard American Diet) is good for no one. I was immediately drawn in, curious to explore the seemingly common sense notion that what we eat affects how we feel. I eliminated white sugar and all animal foods, including dairy from my diet and felt better, almost immediately. My energy stabilized, I woke early feeling well rested. My cravings for sweets seemed to have vanished. I even lost a few extra pounds without trying, although I was eating what seemed like a lot of food. The new foods I tried-beans, grains and unfamiliar vegetables tasted wonderful to me and learning new cooking techniques was a joy. I had found the diet that worked for me and I had no desire to eat or make desserts.

Nevertheless, I did learn that most cravings are based on memories, and cravings are hard to ignore. September farmer's markets, stands piled high with crisp apples, reminded me of my Grandma Ida's cinnamon-scented Fleuden Cake and I longed for a big piece. The filling-jelly scraped from jars, grated tart apples, dried fruit, brown sugar and freshly shelled walnuts (my job), was sandwiched between two pieces of pastry; dough made tender with solid vegetable shortening, glazed with egg and sprinkled with sugar. I had my Grandma's pan, a craving for the cake, a sense of the recipe and a dilemma.

While I wanted Grandma's cake, I did not want to use her ingredients.

I am hardly alone in choosing to eliminate fat-laden, poor quality ingredients from my diet. An ever-expanding, diverse population is heeding the mountains of compelling evidence linking white sugar, hydrogenated fats, dairy and eggs to health problems.

For many, a health crisis, perhaps a heart attack, is the catalyst for dietary change, and foods high in cholesterol, such as meat, milk, butter and eggs are eliminated or restricted.

Other people cite food allergies or intolerance as the deciding factor. Lactose intolerance, the inability to digest milk sugar, is a reality for an estimated sixty to ninety percent of Caucasians and five to fifteen percent of non-Caucasians.

It is compassion for animals that leads vegans (or pure vegetarians) to abstain from all animal foods, including honey and gelatin. Environmental, ethical and religious reasons move others to the same conclusion.

Our motivation is strong and our intentions are clear. Yet, we are loath to give up our favorite foods. No birthday or wedding cakes? No pumpkin pie at Thanksgiving or chocolates on Valentines Day? I do not think that is going to catch on. Do you?

Maybe we just can't help wanting sweets. Our language is sprinkled with sweet words used as metaphors for affection and love. Actually, sweetie, evidence points to a biological predisposition for sweet foods. Scientists speculate earliest man relied on plants for nourishment. The sweeter taste of fruit and roots, life-sustaining, calorie-rich foods may explain the proverbial sweet tooth. Research indicates that of the 5 basic tastes- sweet, sour, bitter, salty and pungent, sweet alone is innately preferred by human babies and mammals.

Deprivation does not work. During my 10 plus years of teaching, I've watched those who never eat dessert and want just a little taste, bingeing on maple syrup in the back of the room. My baking classes are filled with students wishing to enjoy both satisfying desserts and a healthful diet. This ongoing "desserts-can't-live-with-them-can't-live-without-them" conversation, and the disappointing healthy (read: dry) cakes and leaden cookies in the markets, inspired me to try to reinvent the wheel, so to speak. I hit the test kitchen determined to link natural, whole food ingredients with classic technique to create fabulous desserts that just happen to be healthful. This book is the result.

Great Good Desserts Naturally are absolutely delicious and easily made with fresh, seasonal, high quality ingredients. The cakes, creams, fillings and frostings are designed to be mixed and matched. Use the recipes as building blocks and create your own new favorites. *Now, let's go into our kitchens and make something good.*

With all best wishes,
Fran Costigan
New York City, NY
March, 1999.

✳   ✳   ✳

Selected Measures & Equivalents

THIS MEASURE EQUALS	THIS MEASURE	EQUALS THIS MEASURE
3 teaspoons	1 tablespoon	1/2 ounce
4 tablespoons	1/4 cup	2 ounces
5 tablespoons plus 1 teaspoon	1/3 cup	2 1/4 ounces
8 tablespoons	1/2 cup	4 ounces
3/4 cup plus 2 tablespoons	7/8 cup	5 1/3 ounces
16 tablespoons	1 cup	8 ounces
2 cups	1 pint	16 ounces
4 cups	1 quart	32 ounces
1 pound apples	3 cups peeled, cored, sliced	
1 dry pint raspberries	1 1/2 cups (approximate measure)	
1 dry pint strawberries	2 cups (approximate measure)	
1 medium lemon	2 - 3 tablespoons juice	2 to 3 tablespoons zest
1 pound raisins	3 1/2 cups	
1 pound whole almonds	3 1/4 cups	
1/2 cup chocolate chips	1 ounce	

Conventions Used In This Book

	ORGANIC IS ALWAYS PREFERRED
Maple sugar	Granulated evaporated cane juice or organic cane sugar
Maple Syrup	Dark maple syrup (never pancake syrup)
Water	Pure (filtered) water
Pure Vanilla extract	Not vanillin which is artificial vanilla flavoring
Fruit Juice	Unsweetened
Agar	Agar flakes
Jam	Unsweetened, all-fruit jams
Cocoa	Dutch process cocoa (unsweetened)
Carob powder	Roasted and cooled
Chopped nuts	Roasted and cooled
Dried Fruit	Sulfite-free
Oil	Expeller or cold pressed organic canola or hi-oleic safflower oils
Citrus juices	Freshly squeezed
Zest	Finely grated zest from organic fruit
Flours	Whole Wheat Pastry Flour & Unbleached White Flour
Baking Powder	Aluminum free
Salt	Sea salt, fine grind
Spices	Non-irradiated
Soymilk	Vanilla flavored
Ricemilk	Vanilla flavored
Tofu	Firm or extra firm, unless silken is specified
	Tofu is always blanched and pressed prior to use.

FRESH, SEASONAL, ORGANIC INGREDIENTS TASTE BEST AND ARE HEALTH SUPPORTIVE, FOR US, THE FARMERS, THE PLANET

Examples of good quality ingredients are aluminum-free baking powder, sea salt, organic vegetable oils labeled as expeller or cold-pressed, extra virgin olive oil, natural gelatin (agar), arrowroot and kuzu starches, fresh whole grain flours, sugar-free juice and jams, natural sweeteners, sulfite-free dried fruits and pure vanilla and other extracts. All the ingredients used to make the recipes in Great Good Desserts Naturally are real and of good quality. They are available in health food stores, Asian and other ethnic markets, many supermarkets and by mail order.

Despite, the media hype and confusion –what is healthy today might be poison tomorrow– food selection and mealtime need not be a source of stress.

It is quite interesting, shocking really, to learn what's in our food. A good rule is, if you cannot pronounce an ingredient, you should not eat it. Make reading labels a habit, even in health food stores. Author Gail Davis agrees and writes in *So Now What do I Eat?*, "The importance of reading labels cannot be stressed enough."

We are accustomed to finding and eating foods without regard for seasons. Abundant choice may seem wonderful but quite the opposite is true. The trade off is huge and it is dangerous. Food with disappointing taste is the least of the problem. Family farmers cannot compete with agribusiness and farms are lost. Fruits and vegetables are bred to withstand shipping long distances and chemical sprays. These practices waste fuel and pollute the environment.

Mother Nature knows best. Genetically engineered foods, whether vegetable or animal are an insult to nature and endanger everyone's health. Recent reports of butterflies, insects, birds and bees dying after feeding on chemically altered corn are horrific. Mad cow disease is deadly to animals and humans alike. A growth hormone undetectable in milk, iBGH or tBST, is administered to dairy cows "to help them produce more milk." This inhumane practice is of great concern to farmers and consumers alike. Cows are suffering from reproductive problems and infections are on the rise. Furthermore, while there is no definitive data today supporting transmission of the human form of mad cow disease (CJD) through dairy products, many experts consider it probable.

 RGANIC MAKES SENSE

Real food is nourishing and it tastes better too. Imagine going into a market and seeing the conventionally grown foods labeled "grown with poisons and chemicals"? That is the truth, of course. Reasonably priced organic foods is more accessible all the time, thanks to an expanding network of farmer's markets and CSA's (community-supported agriculture). In this win-win situation, farmers have a market for the food they produce, and we have an opportunity to buy good clean food. It is beautiful, really, that what is healthful for us is healthful for the planet.

HAT ARE QUALITY INGREDIENTS?

Utterly satisfying sweets can be thoroughly enjoyed within the context of a healthful diet. The most nourishing foods are whole foods, defined as edible foods as close to their natural state as possible. Examples of whole foods are brown rice and whole grain flours, which retain more of their original parts (vitamins, minerals, fiber) than do white (refined) rice and white flour. It is also important to pay attention to the method and amount of processing a food undergoes.

ORGANIC UNBLEACHED WHITE FLOUR VERSUS STANDARD BLEACHED WHITE FLOUR

Organically grown wheat is milled into white flour gently and without chemicals. Nothing is added to the flour, which is available with the germ intact. On the other hand, standard (supermarket) white flour is refined more completely and enriched with substances such as niacin, thiamine mono-nitrate and iron. Chlorine dioxide, chlorine gas and benzoyl peroxide are used in the whitening (bleaching) process.

While all white flour loses approximately 70 percent of its nutrients during refining, it does substantially lighten whole grain cakes and pastries creating a satisfying result. The baked goods in *Great Good Desserts* contain fifty-percent whole-wheat pastry flour and fifty percent unbleached white flour, in order to create tender nutritionally sound results. Buy whole grain flours from stores with fast turnover and store in the refrigerator or freezer to protect the flours from becoming rancid.

Note that spelt flour, tolerated by many wheat sensitive individuals, can be used in all recipes. No change of measurement is needed. See your health practitioner before experimenting with spelt when allergies to wheat are severe.

USE GOOD QUALITY FATS IN LIMITED AMOUNTS.

Fat is the generic term for butter, margarine, vegetable shortening, lard and oils. The fat of choice in dairy-free baking is neutral flavored organic canola oil. I have used extra-virgin olive oil in strongly flavored cakes such as chocolate, carob and orange with success. Fat phobics should be aware that fat-free baked goods are made with extra sugar, generally have textures like rubber and are not satisfying (to most of us). Eating more is a typical response. Fat-reduced baked goods, on the other hand, made with limited amounts of good quality fat are satisfying and taste good. The fat in all *Great Good* recipes is kept to a minimum, but when circumstances dictate a complete avoidance of fat, choose fruit desserts and jells. They are naturally fat-free and make good eating.

GOOD QUALITY OILS ARE EXTRACTED WITHOUT THE USE OF SOLVENTS OR CHEMICALS.

These oils are light and heat sensitive. Store oils in dark bottles in the refrigerator or freezer. Manufactured (artificial) fats such as margarine taste unpleasant and have been linked to a variety of health problems. Margarine, until recently hailed as the cholesterol-free alternative to butter is actually a liquid (oil), transformed through the process of hydrogenation into solid fat. Hydrogenation creates fake fat known as trans-fat. Our bodies do not recognize trans fatty acids which actually raise levels of (bad)LDL cholesterol and lower (good) HDL cholesterol.

Substitutions & Conversions To Quality Ingredients

INSTEAD OF	USE
Eggs	Tofu, nut butter, fruit puree, kuzu, arrowroot
Baking Powder	Aluminum-free brand such as Rumford
Salt	Sea salt
Cornstarch	Kuzu and Arrowroot
Dairy Milk	Soy, rice, nut, oat "milks"
Buttermilk	Add 2 teaspoons of lemon juice or vinegar to 1 cup soymilk. Set aside for 3 to 5 minutes.
Quick Cooking Oats	Organic rolled oats
All Purpose Flour	Whole wheat pastry flour and unbleached white flour
Butter	Good quality oil, nut butter (1 cup butter = 3/4 cup plus 1 tablespoon oil)
Olive Oil	Extra Virgin Olive Oil
Salad Oil	Vegetable oils, manufactured without chemicals
Solid Shortening	Ice cold, good quality vegetable oils
White Vinegar	Apple Cider and other natural vinegar
Coffee	Organic coffees or grain coffee substitutes
Teas	Organic herbal teas
Dried Fruits	Sulfite-free, sugar-free dried fruits
Bottled Fruit juice	Freshly squeezed or pressed, sugar-free, organic
Jams and Jellies	Sugar-free, all-fruit
Vanilla Flavoring	Pure vanilla extract
Gelatin (Knox)	Agar natural gelatin
Pancake Syrup	Pure maple syrup
White Sugar	Unrefined natural sweeteners, fruit purees

There are better things to spend money on than water. Read the label on a box of low-fat soymilk. Water is the first ingredient. Mix equal amounts of regular soymilk with water and you will have made homemade low-fat soymilk.

HY ORGANIC?

Your food will taste better. You will feel better, the earth will benefit and big businesses will take note.

ATURAL SWEETENERS

The average American consumed more than 130 pounds of sugar in 1991. According to the USDA this includes naturally occurring sugars in fruits, vegetables, milk (lactose), grains and beans. But by far, the largest percentage is the sugar that is added to prepared foods. Breakfast cereals, breads, canned and frozen foods, ketchup, french fries and sodas are foods that are particularly high in sugar. Even non-foods contain sugar or artificial sweeteners. These include toothpaste, table salt and cigarettes. When you read labels and see words ending in "ose" such as high fructose corn syrup and maltose, you have found sugar.

Raw sugar cane contains only 14 percent sucrose before it is refined to 99 percent pure crystalline sucrose, which is one of the simple sugars. This is white table sugar. White sugar, whether from cane or beets has no nutritive value. There is more to the problem of white sugar than just empty calories. It is terribly hard on the body. When simple sugar is consumed, it enters the bloodstream faster than it can be assimilated. The body responds by over-reacting to this, releasing a burst of insulin from the pancreas. The body does a tricky balancing act. Glucose levels drop causing the irritability or fatigue many people experience after eating or drinking sugary foods. The body craves more sugar and the cycle continues. Unlike refined white sugar, natural sweeteners retain some fiber and nutrients, are digested more slowly, processed without chemicals, and may be organically grown.

Vegetarians should note that during processing, sugar might be filtered through bone. Brown sugar is simply refined white sugar with molasses and subject to the same processing. Molasses, a strong tasting sweetener, is a by-product of sugar refining so the chemical residues from processing remain. Organic molasses is now available, however.

Maple sweetener remains the least refined of all the natural sweeteners and has been used as a sweetener for hundreds of years. Maple syrup is nothing more than the boiled sap of maple trees. Maple sugar is evaporated and granulated maple syrup. Native American Indians introduced maple syrup and maple sugar to the colonists. Dubbed Indian Sugar, maple was cheap and remained the primary sweetener until the mid-nineteenth century. During that time, the exorbitant cost of white sugar made it a luxury item, afforded only by the wealthy. Times have changed and the prices of white sugar and maple sweetener have been reversed, but buying maple in bulk quantities (see resource list) lowers the cost considerably. Maple syrup can be stored in the freezer (it does not freeze solid) so fermentation is not an issue.

TWO TYPES OF NATURAL SWEETENERS ARE USED IN THE RECIPES

Dry (Granulated) Sweeteners: Recipes using granulated sweeteners specify maple sugar. However, other natural sweeteners can be substituted and no change of measurement is needed.

1. Maple Sugar
2. Evaporated Cane Juice (Rapadura and Succanat are two popular brands)
3. Organic Sugar Cane (Several brands are marketed)

Liquid sweeteners are specific to the recipes. Substitutions will result in poor, or at least, unpredictable results.

1. Maple Syrup
2. Rice Syrup
3. Barley Malt Syrup
4. Sugar-free Organic Fruit Juices

FOR YOUR INFORMATION

DATE SUGAR: Made from dry dates, date sugar does not dissolve well and is unsuitable for cakes, pies and creams. Use date sugar in crisp toppings and granola. Date sugar burns easily.

HONEY: A food produced by bees, honey is twice as sweet as white sugar. Honey is metabolized very much the same as white sugar and can cause serious fluctuations in blood sugar. Honey should never be fed to children under the age of 2 years because there is a risk of botulism. A vegan diet does not include honey.

CONCENTRATED FRUIT JUICE: Five pounds of fruit are concentrated to make 1 pint of concentrated fruit juice. Nothing of the fruit remains. Concentrated fruit juice is essentially simple sugar. The concentrates are routinely de-ionized to prevent fermentation. This is an example of the importance of considering the type and amount of processing used in food production.

Corn syrup, also known as glucose syrup, is a highly refined food made from cornstarch. High fructose corn syrup is an ingredient in many processed foods. It is cheap to produce and sweeter than sucrose.

Warning! Artificial sweeteners are chemicals and linked to serious health problems including headaches, seizures and blurred vision.

TIPS FOR WORKING WITH NATURAL SWEETENERS

Standard recipes are often too sweet. When converting a conventional recipe, begin by reducing the amount of sweetener 15 to 25 percent.

1. Add a small amount of baking soda to balance the acidity of natural, unrefined sweeteners; 1/4 teaspoon per cup of flour.

2. Natural sweeteners attract water. The increased moistness retards staling and allows for a reduction of fat within a recipe. Potential problems are heavy, sticky or hard baked goods. Reduce liquid or add dry ingredients equal to the amount of liquid sweetener used to replace the granulated (dry) sugar.

3. Measuring heavy, sticky rice syrup and barley malt is easier if you grease the measuring utensil or gently warm the jar of syrup, uncovered, in a pot of simmering water. I prefer the latter method.

4. Extracts and spices add sweetness and flavor. Vanilla and almond extracts, cinnamon, nutmeg, clove and allspice are particularly good choices. Use small amounts; too much spice tastes bitter.

5. Soaked, pureed dried fruits are particularly sweet. Generally, additional sweetener is not needed. Dried fruits are good in fillings, cobblers and crisps.

GUILT-FREE CHOCOLATE &
SOME TALK ABOUT CAROB

The professional baker's secret to converting fat-filled "to die for desserts" into lower fat "chocolate desserts to live for" is substituting unsweetened cocoa powder (10 to 22% fat) for baking chocolate (averaging 54% fat) and there is more good news. The amount of caffeine present in chocolate is tied to the fat, so using lower fat cocoa means a significant reduction in caffeine.

CHOCOLATE IS A BEAN

Mention chocolate and opinions start to fly. Studies indicate phenolic acids present in chocolate (and red wine) provide antioxidant benefits, its stearic acids help raise HDL cholesterol (the good one) and that chocolate boosts serotonin which brightens moods. Pros and cons and studies aside, the consensus remains, chocolate tastes delicious and continues to be one of the most popular foods in the world.

Chocolate comes from beans that grow inside the pods of cacao trees which are among the oldest trees on earth. Chocolate's flavor, color and aroma develop after the beans have been fermented, roasted and ground into a paste. Chocolate liquor (nonalcoholic), an element of the paste, contains a fat called cocoa butter. This is not dairy.

Cocoa is the bitter, dry powder remaining after the chocolate liquor is partially defatted. Cocoa provides a concentrated taste and works beautifully in non-dairy, egg-free recipes. Using unsweetened cocoa means we control the amount and type of sweetener.

Dutch process cocoa (Dutched cocoa), sometimes referred to as European style cocoa, has been treated with an alkaline salt, such as baking soda. It is darker, smoother in flavor and less acidic than natural cocoa. While unprocessed ingredients are always preferred, I find dutched cocoa produces a better result. Natural cocoa requires more sweetener, fat and baking soda, so the two types of cocoa powder can not be used interchangeably.

Pesticides have been routinely used in the production of chocolate but a growing percentage of chocolate is now produced organically by manufacturers who support environmental and economic health of the growers, the consumers and the earth.

THE TO EAT OR NOT TO EAT CHOCOLATE DECISION

I, for one, am not convinced that a chocolate ban is necessary, nor do I think eating chocolate needs to be a sinful pleasure either (unless you find that part of the charm).Individuals with allergies to chocolate or other dietary considerations should do without. Choose organic, non-dairy, naturally sweetened chocolate and don't make chocolate the main course.

AROB IS A POD

Carob, also known as St. John's Bread, like chocolate, comes from the pod of a tropical tree. Chocolate and carob are not generally interchangeable, although many recipes indicate otherwise. Both carob powder and natural cocoa powder are light brown in color. That is where the similarity ends.

> *Carob should be appreciated and savored for its own distinctive, sweet taste.*
> *Do you think tofu tastes like tempeh, or yogurt like heavy cream?*
> *That is what comes to my mind when I am told that carob tastes like chocolate.*

Carob is derived from the dried, roasted, ground pods of the Mediterranean Honey Locust Tree. Carob contains very little fat, is caffeine-free and contains a good dose of calcium and pectin. It has enjoyed a reputation as a food superior to chocolate. However, carob contains more than forty percent naturally occurring sugars. Most importantly, many of the carob confections found in the marketplace contain tropical and hydrogenated oils and sometimes dairy. The fat and sugar content of some manufactured carob candies is as high as ordinary sugar-sweetened, dairy-laden conventional chocolate bars. Read those labels, my fellow consumers, and let the buyer beware.

CAROB DESSERTS TASTE BETTER WHEN MADE WITH ROASTED CAROB

TO ROAST CAROB POWDER
Spread carob on a parchment lined baking pan.
Roast in a 300-degree oven for ten to twelve minutes.
The edges tend to burn. Check carob after six minutes.
You can roast a larger amount of carob than needed.
Store for later use in a tightly closed container.
It will need to be resifted.

SOMETIMES YOU FEEL LIKE A NUT

Store nuts in a covered container or bag in the refrigerator or freezer.
Nuts are high in fat (good quality fat), and can become rancid quickly.

Nuts, seeds, oats and other flakes benefit from light roasting. Their flavor and digestibility are enhanced. Nuts, seeds, oats and other flakes must be cool before they are chopped or ground.

To Roast Nuts
Spread nuts or flakes on a parchment lined baking pan.
Roast in a preheated 325-degree oven for 8 to 12 minutes.
Use a timer. Nuts go from fragrant to burned in seconds.

A GAR A RROWROOT K UZU

WHAT ARE THEY AND HOW DO I USE THEM?

Agar is a natural gelatin that has been used for centuries. Agar is derived from an edible sea vegetable. It is rich in iodine, calcium, phosphorous and trace elements. Agar jells set at room temperature unlike conventional gelatin which must be chilled. Knox gelatin is an example of conventional bovine gelatin. Gelatin is a slaughterhouse by-product derived from collagen, animal hides, skin and crushed bones.

IT IS SIMPLE TO REPLACE STANDARD GELATIN WITH AGAR.
Agar is available in three forms: flakes, bars and powder.

SUBSTITUTIONS TO REMEMBER
To convert a recipe from gelatin to agar:
Use three times as much agar as the gelatin listed in the recipe.

> 3 teaspoons agar flakes = 1 teaspoon gelatin
>
> 1 teaspoon gelatin jells 1 cup liquid
>
> 3 teaspoons agar flakes jells 1 cup liquid
>
> (3 teaspoons = 1 tablespoon)
>
> 4 tablespoons agar flakes = 1 bar agar

Agar bars are soaked in cold water, squeezed dry, shredded into the specified liquid and cooked until agar is dissolved, 5 to 10 minutes after the boil.

SOME TIPS TO REMEMBER
When citrus is an ingredient, 10 to 20 percent more agar might be needed.

Agar flakes dissolve more easily during cooking after a brief soak.
Pour the liquid specified in the recipe into a pot and sprinkle agar flakes onto the surface. Do not stir or heat. Allow agar to soften for 10 minutes before cooking.

Agar can be reheated which is a plus when it is necessary to adjust the texture of a prepared jell.

The basic recipe for agar is Fruit Jell-O, found on page 36.

KUZU & ARROWROOT ARE STARCHES

Starches are valued friends of the dairy-free dessert maker.
Kuzu and arrowroot, like other forms of starch, thicken liquids.
In addition, they add a creamy texture, usually contributed by eggs.

KUZU (KUDZU) STARCH, derived from the root of the kuzu (kudzu) plant, is considered soothing to digestive and circulatory systems so a kuzu-thickened dessert is a good choice after a heavy meal. Interesting new research indicates kuzu may reduce cravings for alcohol. Kuzu is an expensive ingredient but small quantities are used, and kuzu sold in bulk bins is much less expensive option than the little packages. Do, however, buy kuzu from a reputable company. If the price is too good to be true, the kuzu has probably been mixed with potato flour.

ARROWROOT, ARROWROOT FLOUR AND ARROWROOT POWDER are the same ingredient. Arrowroot is derived from the starch of a plant native to the West Indies. Arrowroot does not have the medicinal properties attributed to kuzu, but it is a highly digestible natural ingredient. Arrowroot is available in ethnic markets and health food stores. The small bottles available in the supermarket are terribly expensive.

SUBSTITUTIONS TO REMEMBER

Use two times as much arrowroot as kuzu.

2 teaspoons arrowroot = 1 teaspoon kuzu.

2 teaspoons arrowroot = 2 teaspoons cornstarch

Cornstarch is highly refined and not recommended.

SOME TIPS TO REMEMBER

When citrus is an ingredient, 5 to 15 percent more starch might be needed.

All starches must be dissolved in cool water prior to cooking. This is called a slurry.

Arrowroot and kuzu slurries are stirred into a hot liquid, but the cooking method for each starch is different.

Dissolved arrowroot is added to a liquid and stirred continuously but not vigorously. It is cooked only to, or a few seconds after a boil is reached. Arrowroot thins if it is cooked too long or stirred too much.

Dissolved kuzu, on the other hand, must be cooked for 1 or 2 minutes after a boil is reached to stabilize the starch and stirring is not an issue. In both cases, the mixture is expected to thicken and become clear.

LETS TALK TOFU

TOFU, A SOY PRODUCT MADE FROM SOYMILK, IS SOMETIMES REFERRED TO AS THE VEGETABLE COW. It is a boon to bakers and cooks alike. The benefits of eating soy foods have been universally accepted.

Tofu is a nutritious, affordable, widely available and versatile food.
It is, however, perishable and when stored in unsanitary or warm conditions can harbor dangerous bacteria. To be certain your tofu is fresh and safe, select organic tofu from the refrigerated section, not the (too warm) produce section of your market and check the pull dates on the packages. Never purchase tofu sold from open tubs. While it makes sense to reduce packaging, safety issues such as quality of the water and bacteria introduced by unsanitary hands and utensils make purchasing unwrapped, bulk tofu too great a risk.

Soybeans are routinely sprayed with toxic chemicals and are being genetically engineered. It is important to buy tofu and other soy products processed from organically grown soybeans.

Blanching and pressing tofu before it is used assures a safe, more digestible food and because the water content is greatly reduced, a consistent result is assured. Silken tofu is not blanched. Instead, it is steamed in a steamer basket. Silken tofu is not pressed.

BLANCHING TOFU

Unwrap and rinse the tofu. Submerge the tofu in a pot of fresh water. Bring water to a boil, reduce heat and simmer 10 minutes. Use a slotted spoon or strainer to lift the tofu out of the water. Wrap blanched tofu in clean white kitchen towels or paper toweling and squeeze lightly. Tofu that has been blanched can be safely stored in a covered container in the refrigerator for 3 or 4 days.

PRESSING TOFU

Wrap blanched tofu in several towels, place the package directly on your countertop or on a tray and weight it with a heavy object (an unopened box of soymilk, a book or heavy skillet) for 10 minutes. To press a larger amount of tofu, place wrapped tofu on a cutting board or flat tray and cover with another board or tray. Place the edge of the board over the rim of the sink. Slip a book or something else that will raise the board about 15 degrees under its bottom and let the water drain into the sink.

Tofu is available packaged in water (organic) and in aseptic boxes (non-organic)

SILKEN   SOFT   FIRM   EXTRA-FIRM

QUALITY COOKWARE & EQUIPAMENT

HEALTHY BAKING DOES NOT REQUIRE FANCY EQUIPMENT.

My big electric mixer sits on a shelf, replaced by bowls and hand whisks.

Aluminum cookware is widely used in the food service industry, despite the fact that aluminum contamination has been linked to a wide range of health problems. Better choices for cooks are stainless steel (a layer of aluminum sandwiched on the bottom is common and desirable), tinned steel, glass and ceramic pie plates and baking dishes and enameled and plain cast iron. Similarly, aluminum foil should not touch food directly. Use it only as over-wrap.

Purchasing good quality pots, pans and tools is well worth the cost. They perform better and make cooking and baking a pleasure. Using inadequate tools is frustrating and can spoil your efforts. Heavy cookie sheets and baking pans do not warp in a hot oven and pots with heavy bottoms help to keep foods from scorching. Excellent quality pots and pans go on sale several times a year.

USE THE CORRECT SIZE BAKING PANS.

THE AMOUNT OF BATTER IN A CAKE PAN IS NOT NEGOTIABLE. Too little batter in too large a pan means a cake that is dry and thin. A cracker is probably not what you had in mind. Too much batter in too small a pan yields a cake that does not cook through. The center will be wet, gummy and most likely collapse.

It is safe to assume that unless the recipe indicates otherwise, the proper volume of dairy/egg-free batter is one-third to a scant half the depth of the pan. Cakes are expected to rise.

In order to substitute one baking pan for another, the volume of the new pan must be measured. You can determine the volume of any pan by using a liquid measuring cup filled with water to fill the pan. Pans are measured across the top from rim to rim.

A ROUND CAKE PAN HOLDS ONLY 3/4 OF THE VOLUME AS THE SAME SIZE SQUARE PAN.

Therefore, the pans are not the same size.

9-inch round pan holds 6 to 6 1/2 cups batter to full capacity.

>> USE 2 TO 3 CUPS BATTER.

9 x 9-inch square pan holds 8 to 9 cups to full capacity.

>> USE 3 TO 4 CUPS BATTER.

9 x 13-inch pan (sheet cake) hold 16 cups batter to full capacity.

>> USE 6 TO 8 CUPS BATTER.

9-inch heart shape pan holds about 5 cups to full capacity.

>> USE 2 TO 2 1/2 CUPS BATTER.

BAKING EQUIPMENT

Everything you need to make and bake all the recipes in this book is on this list.
Buy individual items as needed, but remember, buy cheap, buy trouble.

Paring knives	Choose what feels comfortable to hold.
Chef's knife	9 or 10-inch (keep your knives sharp)
Serrated knife	Also called baker's knife
Cutting boards	Wood, dedicated to desserts (no garlic)
Kitchen scissors	
Vegetable peelers	
Fine mesh strainers	Instead of sifters
Saucepans and covers	1, 2, 3, 8 quart sizes
Measuring cups and spoons	Liquid and dry measures
Mixing bowls	Small, medium, large, stainless steel and glass
Flexible rubber spatulas	Small, medium, large
Wire whisks	Small, medium, large
Mixing spoons	Stainless steel and wood
Zester	
Pastry brushes	For oiling pans and glazing baked goods
Cake testers or skewers	
Wire (cake) cooling racks	Rounds, squares and a large rectangle
Offset metal spatulas	Small and medium
Rolling pin	A heavy pin with ball bearing handle
Food processor	
Oven thermometer	Mercury thermometers are accurate
Oven timer	Triple timers are invaluable
Parchment paper	Also called baker's paper. Available unbleached
12 cup muffin tin	
8-inch square baking pans	
9-inch square baking pans	
8-inch round cake pans	
9-inch round cake pans and 9-inch springform pans	
8-inch tart pan with removable bottom	
8-inch pie plate	
9 x 13-inch baking pan	
Cookie sheets	Are rimless
Baking sheet pans	Also called jellyroll pans
Kitchen towels	
Oven mitts	
Storage containers	
Food wrap and bags	
Cake and pie servers, blender, cake-decorating turntable, cardboard cake circles	

ABOUT FLOURS

ALL WHEAT CONTAINS A PROTEIN KNOWN AS GLUTEN. Gluten develops when liquid and flour are mixed and it creates structure. Whole wheat flour contains considerably more protein than whole wheat pastry flour. Consequently, whole wheat pastry flour is the best choice for baking dessert, while whole-wheat flour is best for baking bread. Whole-wheat pastry flour and unbleached white flour in a fifty-fifty ratio is the best formula for creating tender cakes and other baked goods. Purchase flour from shops with fast turnover and store in covered containers or bags, in the refrigerator or freezer. Cold protects the oils in the germ remaining in whole grain flours from becoming rancid.

FOR ACCURACY, ALL INGREDIENTS MUST BE CAREFULLY MEASURED WITH THE APPROPRIATE MEASURING TOOLS

In order to achieve excellent and consistent results in baking,
flour, leavening and liquids must be precisely measured.

MEASURE DRY INGREDIENTS: A set of dry measuring cups (including 1/4, 1/3, 1/2 and 1 cup) is indispensable and a heavyweight, straight-sided set is best. Dip a cup into the flour or cocoa or sweetener and scoop the ingredient into the cup. Fill to overflowing and sweep the dull edge of a knife across the top to level. Do not press down, shake or bang the cup, as this will change the measurement. Use measuring spoons with the same dip, scoop and sweep method to measure small quantities of dry ingredients such as baking powder, baking soda, spices and sea salt. Don't use fancy shaped measures or spoons from your set of dinnerware!

WET OR LIQUID INGREDIENTS: Measure in clear glass or plastic cups marked in increments. This type of cup has a pouring spout. The most useful sizes are 1, 2 and 4 cup measures and larger ones are handy. For accuracy, place cups on a level surface to measure liquids. Wet and dry measuring tools hold different amounts and are not interchangeable.

SIFT THE DRY INGREDIENTS. You want a tender cake, right? I use a fine mesh strainer to sift because the bran in whole grain flours gets stuck in triple mesh sifters. After the dry ingredients are sifted into the bowl, mix and aerate them with a wire whisk.

WET INGREDIENTS ARE POURED INTO DRY INGREDIENTS. Mix with a wire whisk only until batter is smooth. Dairy-free (vegan) batters are generally thinner than standard egg-butter batters and should not fill more than half the depth of the pan, unless a particular recipe indicates otherwise. With practice, you will learn to recognize just the right consistency. Keep wet and dry ingredients separate and never combine them until you are sure you are ready to take that filled pan directly to the oven. This means your oven is preheated, your pans are oiled and lined, and your timer is at hand. If the cake batter sits around, the leavening provided by the baking powder and baking soda is finished before you start. You do not have to run to your oven, but do not let the batter hang out on the counter either.

CAKES ARE BAKED IN THE CENTER OF THE OVEN.

Cakes must cool on wire cooling racks, generally 10 minutes in the pan, then turned out of the pan to finish cooling.

Plan ahead, cold cake layers are easier to divide into thinner layers, to fill and to frost. Cake layers can be baked in advance, wrapped tightly and refrigerated or frozen. Defrost cakes, still wrapped, in the refrigerator. Any condensation that occurs will stay on the wrap, not the cake.

Cupcakes can be made with cake batters. Oil cupcake tins well but do not use paper liners for non-dairy batters. The baking time may be shorter. Check cupcakes after 15 minutes.

PIES AND TARTS ARE BAKED IN THE LOWER THIRD OF THE OVEN.

Pies, like cakes need to be thoroughly cooled after baking on wire cooling racks.

Fruit pies in particular need time for the juices to thicken.

Warm pies, if you like, in a 300-degree oven before serving.

WIRE COOLING RACKS ARE PART OF THE PROCESS.

The racks elevate baking pans, allowing air to circulate. This step is important to guard against soggy bottoms on pies and cakes.

NOTES _____

_____

_____

_____

_____

_____

_____

_____

_____

_____

_____

_____

_____

_____

_____

_____

NOTES

Chapter 2

Dreamy, Creamy

puddings & jells, mousses, custards & more

The rich, smooth and airy texture associated with this type of dessert is traditionally created by using heavy cream, milk and eggs, plus gelatin and white sugar – ingredients that have no place in healthful desserts.

The secret to making just-as-delicious-maybe-better-versions is non-dairy milks, tofu, kuzu and arrowroot starch, natural gelatin (agar) and natural sweeteners.

The results are .... dreamy, creamy and honestly great.

Healthy Desserts 101
dreamy, creamy
a short review

Arrowroot and kuzu are starches that thicken and cream. These ingredients create the texture we expect from pudding and mousse type desserts. The starches are interchangeable. It is, however, necessary to use twice as much arrowroot as kuzu. Agar is a natural gelatin. Use 3 times as much agar as commercial gelatin. Tofu is extremely versatile; it makes frostings, creams, whipped toppings and more. A combination of starch, natural gelatin and tofu is often used in recipes.

STARCHES MUST BE DISSOLVED IN COOL WATER PRIOR TO COOKING. THIS IS CALLED A SLURRY. Starch thickened foods should be brought to a gentle boil over low heat. Starches are semi-crystalline granules that release starch when they are heated to a boil. Arrowroot is cooked only to, or a few seconds after it boils and is stirred gently. Kuzu must cook 1 to 2 minutes after the boil is reached to stabilize the starch. It can be stirred without worry of thinning. Kuzu thickened desserts do not cloud or thin, even after 1 or 2 days.

AGAR IS A NATURAL GELATIN DERIVED FROM SEA VEGETABLES (SEAWEED). Agar jells are very stable and set at room temperature, usually in 2 to 3 hours. The time is considerably shorter, 45 minutes to 1 hour, when jells are refrigerated. Agar dissolves more easily during cooking when it is softened in cool liquid 10 minutes prior to cooking.

TOFU IS A SOY FOOD PRODUCED FROM SOYMILK. Tofu replaces eggs and whipped cream and is used to makes creams that can be piped though pastry bags. Tofu should be blanched and pressed before it is used.

Detailed information about these ingredients is found on pages 24 to 26 .

The Recipes

FRUIT JELL-O

BLUEBERRY JELL

FRUIT SOUP & SALAD

SILKEN CASHEW CREAM

TROPICAL FRUIT MOUSSE

MY T GOOD CHOCOLATE PUDDING

CHOCOLATE SHERBET-SORBET

MAPLE GINGER, ALMOND & HAZELNUT CREAMS

LET THEM EAT BREAD PUDDING

TASTES LIKE IT COULD BE HARD SAUCE

CREAMY BROWN RICE & RAISIN PUDDING

MAPLE CIDER SAUCE

 RUIT JELL-O

6 TO 8 SERVINGS

A variety of 'Jello' preparations are showing up on menus again! Make better Jell-O by replacing conventional bovine gelatin with agar, a calorie free and mineral rich sea vegetable. Agar jells, also called kantens, set up at room temperature but refrigerating jells shortens the process. Kuzu and arrowroot are good quality root starches that thicken and add creamy texture. Agar, kuzu and arrowroot are readily available in health food stores, Asian and other ethnic markets and larger supermarkets.

GETTING STARTED
Medium pot with cover

INGREDIENTS
4 cups apple juice or other sugar-free fruit juice
4 tablespoons agar flakes
Pinch sea salt
1/2 teaspoon ground nutmeg or mace
2 teaspoons kuzu or 4 teaspoon of arrowroot dissolved in 4 teaspoons water
1 1/2 cups sliced fruit

1. Pour the juice into a medium pot and sprinkle agar flakes onto surface of juice. Do not stir or heat. Allow agar to soften for 10 minutes.

2. Add sea salt and spice to the softened agar. Cover pot and bring juice and agar to a boil over medium heat. Uncover, reduce heat and simmer until agar is completely dissolved, stirring occasionally, 5 to 10 minutes. Remove a tablespoon of liquid from the pot and check jell for any specks of agar that have not dissolved. Continue if necessary to simmer until agar has completely melted into the juice.

3. Test the jell: Refrigerate 1 tablespoon of jell for 5 to 10 minutes until it sets. If the jell is too soft, cool the liquid in the pot, add more agar flakes and simmer until agar dissolves. If it is too firm, add more liquid.

4. Add the dissolved starch (kuzu or arrowroot) to the jell stirring constantly and cook over low heat until the mixture boils. Reduce heat and cook kuzu 1 to 2 minutes longer. Cook arrowroot only until a boil is reached; the mixture will thin if it is cooked too long. The mixture will be cloudy at first, but as it thickens it will clear.

5. Pour the juice mixture into a shallow dish and cool 15 minutes or until slightly thickened. Stir in fruit and refrigerate until jell is set, 45 minutes to 1 hour.

GOOD BAKER'S TIPS & VARIATIONS
Remember to test jells. Add more agar flakes or more juice to fix jells that are too soft or too firm. I have found Eden brand agar flakes to be extremely reliable.

To make a simpler jell-o, eliminate the arrowroot or kuzu.

BLUEBERRY JELL

6 TO 8 SERVINGS

This jell, slighter softer than Fruit Jell-O, has an especially beautiful color.

GETTING STARTED
   Medium pot with cover
   Food processor or blender

INGREDIENTS
   4 cups apple or (other sugar-free) juice
   1/2 teaspoon ground cinnamon
   Pinch sea salt
   3 tablespoons agar flakes
   2 cups blueberries, picked over, washed and patted dry
   1 tablespoon kuzu or 2 tablespoons arrowroot dissolved in 2 tablespoons water
   1/2 teaspoon vanilla extract

1. Follow the recipe for Fruit Jell-O on page 36. Stir in blueberries after step 3, just before the starch is added.

2. Refrigerate jell until it has set, 45 minutes to 1 hour, then cream jell in a food processor. Apple juice 'beige' becomes a beautiful natural, bright blue.

GOOD BAKERS TIPS & VARIATIONS
Frozen organic berries can replace fresh berries but cook them a few minutes longer.

Puree a portion of jell with more juice (and maple syrup to taste) in a blender or food processor for a jewel-like fruit sauce.

Serve jell plain or create a parfait by layering plain jell, creamed jell, fruit sauce and granola or cake crumbs.

AN E-MAIL FROM SEATTLE
   Fran, You have introduced me to jells. Thank you! I have always hated jello with a passion, and when I became a vegan, was glad to have that behind me. Then, I discovered that several vegan chefs use agar to jell liquid, and I thought, Oh boy, who needs that? BUT, when I tasted your jell with the nut cream (handed out at the demo) I was amazed and delighted.
   LARRISA

   Thank you Larrisa, the next recipe is dedicated to you.

 Fruit Soup & Salad

6 TO 8 SERVINGS

A softly jelled fruit soup served with a salad of figs and blueberries adapted from Molly O'Neill's recipe previously published in the New York Times, this intentionally soft jell is elegant, wheat-free, sugar-free and fat-free.

GETTING STARTED
Medium pot with cover
Suggestion: Silken Cashew Cream (page 39)

INGREDIENTS- FRUIT SOUP
> 4 cups apple or other sugar-free juice
> 1/4 teaspoon sea salt
> 2 1/2 tablespoons agar flakes
> 1/2 teaspoon vanilla extract
>> OPTIONAL AROMATICS: VANILLA BEAN, CINNAMON STICK, FRESH GINGER, STAR ANISE

INGREDIENTS- FRUIT SALAD
> 2 cups fresh blueberries, picked over, washed and patted dry
> 4 fresh figs, washed, halved or quartered
> 1 to 2 tablespoons maple sugar
> 1/4 teaspoon mace or nutmeg
> 1 tablespoon grated orange zest
>> OPTIONAL: 1 TO 2 TABLESPOONS GRAND MARNIER
>> GARNISH: LONG, THIN STRIPS OF ORANGE ZEST

FRUIT SOUP
1. Pour juice into a pot and sprinkle agar flakes onto surface of juice. Do not stir or heat and allow agar to soften for 10 minutes.

2. Add salt and optional aromatics, cover pot and bring juice to a boil over medium heat. Uncover pot, reduce heat and cook 5 to 10 minutes, stirring occasionally, until agar is dissolved. Remove the pot from the stove and add vanilla. Pour the juice mixture into a shallow dish. Refrigerate until set, 45 minutes to 1 hour.

FRUIT SALAD
1. Combine the blueberries, figs, maple sugar, grated orange zest and optional Grand Marnier in a shallow bowl and mix gently. Set fruit aside at room temperature while jell sets. The fruit will release juice into the bowl; this is just fine.

TO SERVE
Spoon a portion of fruit soup into individual dessert bowls. Top each serving with Fruit Salad and accumulated juices. Garnish with Silken Cashew Cream and strips of orange zest.

GOOD BAKERS TIPS & VARIATIONS
Residues from pesticides that are routinely sprayed on fruit are hazardous to health.
Omit zest from the recipe when non-organic fruit is used.

SILKEN CASHEW CREAM

1 TO 1 1/2 CUPS

Rich in taste and texture only, this indispensable rice syrup sweetened nut cream transforms simple fruits into stylish desserts, enlivens shortcake, and elegantly finishes cobblers, crisps, puddings and jells.

GETTING STARTED
Food processor

INGREDIENTS
1 cup cashews, very lightly toasted, cooled
1/4 teaspoon sea salt
1/3 to 1/2 cup rice syrup, warmed
1 tablespoon vanilla extract
1/4 teaspoon almond extract
1/4 to 1/2 cup filtered water

1. Grind nuts to a fine meal in a food processor. Add salt. Add rice syrup in 2 additions and continue to process until mixture is smooth. Stop the processor a few times and scrape down the sides. Add extracts and the smaller amount of water; process until nut cream is absolutely smooth. This will take 2 to 3 minutes or longer. Add more water to adjust consistency.

2. Refrigerate the nut cream in a covered container. Nut cream stays fresh up to 2 weeks but thickens when cold. Thin with water as needed.

GOOD BAKER'S TIPS & VARIATIONS
Other roasted nuts, including blanched almonds, skinned hazelnuts and pecans make beautiful creams. I have found walnuts bitter.

Keep a container of nut cream in your freezer, it will stay fresh for up to 1 month. Spoon what you need out of the container. Nut cream defrosts very fast.

TROPICAL FRUIT MOUSSE

6 TO 8 SERVINGS

The following recipe was previously published in DELICIOUS! Magazine and was one of the most requested dessert recipes ever. Dried fruit, silken tofu and fruit juice combine to create a creamy mousse. Drying fruit intensifies its natural sweetness, making additional sweeteners unnecessary. Mousse blended with extra juice = great sauce. It is easiest to cut dried fruit with scissors. A luscious tart is made by spreading mango mousse into a baked and cooled tart crust such as the crust on page 109.

GETTING STARTED
Medium saucepan
Food processor

INGREDIENTS
4 ounces dried sugar-free mango
2 ounces dried sugar-free pineapple
2 to 3 cups sugar-free mango juice or apple juice, divided
1 1/2 cups tofu, blanched and pressed
1 small ripe banana, peeled and sliced
1 tablespoon orange juice
1/4 cup agar flakes
1/2 teaspoon lemon extract
1 tablespoon kuzu or 2 tablespoons arrowroot, dissolved in 3 tablespoons water
GARNISHES: FRESH FRUIT, TOASTED COCONUT, MANGO PUREE

1. Put mango and pineapple into separate small bowls. Heat 2 cups mango juice to a boil in a medium saucepan and pour one cup hot juice into each bowl of fruit. Soak the fruit for at least 10 minutes or up to a day in advance.

2. Puree softened mango with soaking juice in food processor. Set aside 2 tablespoons of mango puree for garnish. Leave the rest in the food processor.

3. Drain the pineapple; reserve juice and set aside to cool. Add pineapple, tofu, banana and orange juice to mango puree and process until mixture is creamy.

4. Add enough juice or water to the pineapple soaking liquid to measure 1 1/4 cups. Pour juice into the saucepan and sprinkle agar flakes onto the surface. Do not stir or heat. Allow agar to soften for 10 minutes.

5. Cover pot and bring juice and agar to a boil over medium heat. Uncover, reduce heat and simmer until agar is completely dissolved, 5 to 10 minutes. Whisk in dissolved kuzu or arrowroot starch stirring constantly. Cook until mixture returns to a boil, thickens and clears. Cook kuzu 1 to 2 minutes after the boil; arrowroot only to the boil.

6. Remove pot from the stove, add lemon extract and spoon mixture into food processor. Process until mousse is smooth. Spoon into a shallow dish, cover and refrigerate until the mousse sets, 30 minutes to 1 hour. The mousse can be made 24 hours before serving.

7. Cream mousse in a food processor about 30 minutes before serving; pulse the machine 8 to 10 times. Spoon the mousse into serving dishes and garnish.

My T Good Chocolate Pudding

6 TO 8 SERVINGS

Delicious served warm or at room temperature, chocolate pudding is, for chocoholics, a basic food group. Here agar flakes and kuzu provide the creamy texture without adding a drop of fat. This pudding makes a fine pie filling too.

GETTING STARTED
Medium pot with cover

INGREDIENTS
2 cups water, divided
2 tablespoons agar flakes
1/2 cup Dutch process cocoa
1 cup vanilla soymilk or ricemilk
1/4 teaspoon sea salt
1 cup maple syrup
2 tablespoons kuzu or 1/4 cup arrowroot dissolved in 1/2 cup water
1 tablespoon vanilla extract

1. Pour 1 cup of water into a medium pot. Sprinkle agar flakes over the water and allow agar to soften for 10 minutes without stirring or heating. Cover the pot and bring water and agar flakes to a boil over medium heat. Uncover, reduce heat to low and cook 5 to 10 minutes, stirring occasionally, until agar is dissolved.

2. Sift cocoa onto a piece of waxed paper. Add the cocoa to the pot, stirring until chocolate dissolves. Add soymilk or ricemilk, the second cup of water, salt and maple syrup to the pot, stirring until the mixture is smooth and hot. Whisk dissolved kuzu or arrowroot starch into the chocolate, stirring constantly and cook until mixture comes to a boil, thickens and clears. Cook kuzu for 1 to 2 minutes after the boil; cook arrowroot only to the boil.

3. Remove the pot from the stove and add vanilla. Pour the pudding into a serving bowl or into individual dishes.

GOOD BAKER'S TIPS & VARIATIONS

MINT CHOCOLATE PUDDING:
Add 1/4 teaspoon of mint extract.
Mint extract has a very strong tast. Add it cautiously.
Too much extract makes the pudding taste like medicine.
I know that from personal experience.

CHOCOLATE SHERBERT-SORBET

6 SERVINGS

While sorbet is the French translation of sherbet, they now refer to different foods. Sorbet is dairy-free and contains no gelatin; sherbet contains egg whites, milk and gelatin.

GETTING STARTED
Medium pot with cover

INGREDIENTS
1 cup water
2 tablespoons agar flakes
1/2 cup Dutch process cocoa
1 cup vanilla soymilk or ricemilk
1/4 teaspoon sea salt
3/4 cup maple syrup
1 tablespoon kuzu or 2 tablespoons arrowroot dissolved in 1/2 cup water
1 tablespoon vanilla extract
1/4 teaspoon almond extract

1. Pour water into a medium pot. Sprinkle agar flakes over the water and allow agar to soften for 10 minutes without stirring or heating. Cover the pot and bring water and agar flakes to a boil over medium heat. Uncover pot, reduce heat to low and cook 5 to 10 minutes, stirring occasionally, until agar is dissolved.

2. Sift cocoa onto a piece of waxed paper. Add cocoa to the pot, stirring until mixture is smooth. Add the soymilk or ricemilk, salt and maple syrup to the chocolate mixture. Whisk dissolved kuzu or arrowroot starch into the hot chocolate mixture, stirring constantly and cook until mixture comes to a boil, thickens and clears. Cook kuzu for 1 to 2 minutes after the boil; cook arrowroot only to the boil. Remove the pot from the stove and add extracts. Pour the hot chocolate mixture into a shallow dish and cool. Cover and chill in refrigerator.

3.   If using an ice cream machine, follow manufacturers directions. Alternatively, freeze in covered container and cream in food processor prior to serving.

ON WOMEN CRAVING CHOCOLATE
Women are often deficient in magnesium and chocolate contains magnesium. Women are the largest consumers of chocolate. Might cravings for chocolate be the body's way of looking for magnesium-rich foods? Or, are women conditioned to enjoy chocolate because chocolates are so often given as gifts? Researchers are looking at issues such as these at this time and the studies are interesting, but there is no question that we should count on grains, beans and vegetables as the optimal sources of magnesium and eat good quality dairy-free chocolate

MAPLE GINGER CREAM

6 SERVINGS

The flavor of this tofu cream compliments many desserts. Use it to fill and frost cakes or as a topping for fresh or dried fruit. Make different flavored tofu creams following this basic recipe; add jam, fruit puree icings, nut cream, whole berries and more. To make ginger juice, grate peeled fresh ginger, then press hard on the solids.

GETTING STARTED
   Food processor or blender

INGREDIENTS
   1 pound box firm tofu, blanched and pressed
   1/4 cup smooth cashew butter or 2 tablespoons canola oil
   3/4 cup maple syrup
   1/4 cup maple sugar
   1 teaspoon sea salt
   1 teaspoon ground ginger
   2 to 3 tablespoons fresh ginger juice
   1 tablespoon vanilla extract
   1/4 teaspoon orange extract

1.   Cream tofu in food processor or blender. Add remaining ingredients and blend until tofu mixture is very smooth and creamy. Refrigerate cream tightly covered at least 1 hour or up to 24 hours to allow flavors to blend.

ALMOND CREAM
Follow the recipe for Maple Ginger Cream. Substitute almond butter for the cashew butter. Eliminate ground ginger, ginger juice, orange extract. Add 1 teaspoon almond extract. Stir chopped or ground almonds or Silken Cashew Cream (page 39), made with almonds into the tofu cream.

HAZELNUT CREAM
Follow the recipe for Almond Cream.
Use hazelnut butter instead of almond butter. Add finely ground, toasted hazelnuts. The combination of chocolate and hazelnut is especially scrumptious. Fold chocolate glaze or frosting into hazelnut cream, one tablespoon at a time until the taste works for you.

GOOD BAKER'S TIPS & VARIATIONS
To make ginger juice, peel the ginger and rub one end up and down on a fine grater. Squeeze the grated ginger, a handful at a time, over a small bowl. Discard the pulp. Alternatively, cut ginger into small pieces. Turn on a food processor and add ginger through the feed tube. Process until ginger is grated. This is a good method for preparing a larger quantity of ginger juice. Stir ginger juice before using.

LET THEM EAT BREAD PUDDING

8 TO 10 SERVINGS

An honest bread pudding made better with natural ingredients. Fruit is mixed into this pudding, based on a recipe developed by the late great chef Frank Acuri.

GETTING STARTED
Preheated 350 degree oven
Oiled 9 x 13 inch-baking dish or equivalent
SUGGESTION: SERVE WITH 'TASTES LIKE IT COULD BE HARD SAUCE '(PAGE 45)

INGREDIENTS
1 pound dense, whole grain bread, thickly sliced (stale is fine)
2 cups water
2 cups vanilla soymilk
1 cup apple or pear juice
3/4 cup raisins, soaked in 1/2 cup orange juice
1/4 cup maple syrup
1/4 teaspoon sea salt
2 teaspoons ground cinnamon
1/2 teaspoon ground mace
1/4 teaspoon ground cloves
2 teaspoons vanilla extract
1 teaspoon almond extract
2 tablespoons kuzu or 4 tablespoons arrowroot, dissolved in 4 tablespoons juice
2 cups chopped fruit: apple, pear, banana
3/4 cup pecans, toasted, cooled and chopped, divided

1. Put the bread into a large bowl and cover with water. Soak bread 5 minutes to soften but don't let bread disintegrate. Drain the bread in a colander. Dry the bowl and return bread to the bowl. Drain the raisins, saving the orange juice.

2. Mix the soymilk, fruit juice and orange juice, maple syrup, salt, spices, extracts and dissolved kuzu or arrowroot in a bowl and pour over the bread. Stir in the chopped fruit, raisins and half the nuts and mix well.

3. Spoon the bread pudding into the baking dish. Cover the top with parchment paper and over wrap with foil. Bake the pudding for 20 minutes; remove foil and bake 10 minutes longer.

4. Serve bread pudding warm or at room temperature with Hard Sauce (page 45) and sprinkle each serving with some of the remaining nuts.

GOOD BAKER'S TIPS & VARIATIONS
Let Them Eat Bread Pudding and Tastes Like It Could Be Hard Sauce is a match made in heaven but frozen non-dairy frozen desserts, store bought or home made, melting on top of a bowl of warm pudding makes me smile too. *Chocolate Bread Pudding is unsuitable for breakfast but delicious nonetheless*: Add chips or chunks of non-dairy chocolate to the pudding before it is baked.

Tastes Like it Could be Hard Sauce

2 CUPS

But it's not. Hard Sauce, also called Whiskey sauce, is a popular accompaniment to bread pudding. The conventional recipe calls for 1 stick of butter, 2 eggs, 1 cup of whiskey and sugar. This better for you version is great.

GETTING STARTED
Medium pot

INGREDIENTS
2 cups apple or pear juice
1/2 cup soymilk
1 to 2 tablespoons mirin (or whiskey)
1 tablespoon kuzu or 2 tablespoons arrowroot, dissolved in 2 tablespoons orange juice or water
2 teaspoons vanilla extract
1 teaspoon almond extract
1/2 teaspoon orange extract

1. Cook fruit juice slowly, uncovered, in medium pot until it reduces by half. Add soymilk and mirin to the juice and simmer 2 to 3 minutes longer. Add dissolved kuzu, or arrowroot starch, stirring constantly. Cook 1 to 2 minutes after the boil if using kuzu;, cook arrowroot only to the boil. Remove the pot from the stove and add extracts.

GOOD BAKER'S TIPS & VARIATIONS
Mirin is Japanese sweet rice cooking wine.
"Let Them Eat Hard Sauce" is tasty poured over rice pudding, and non-dairy frozen desserts too.

CREAMY BROWN RICE & RAISIN PUDDING

4 CUPS

A great tasting comfort food, packed with healthy ingredients, rice pudding makes a perfectly nourishing breakfast as well as a sensible end to a light meal. Cook extra rice, store it in a covered container in your refrigerator and make rice pudding in a flash.

GETTING STARTED
Preheated 375 degree oven
Oiled 1 1/2 quart baking dish
Food processor

INGREDIENTS
2 cups cooked brown rice
1 cup ricemilk or soymilk, plus additional for serving
1 1/2 cups firm tofu, blanched
1/3 cup rice syrup
1/4 cup maple syrup
2 teaspoons ground cinnamon
1/2 teaspoon ground nutmeg
1 tablespoon kuzu or 2 tablespoons arrowroot, dissolved in 2 tablespoons water
2 teaspoons vanilla extract
2/3 cup raisins
2/3 cup roasted sunflower seeds
1 teaspoon ground cinnamon mixed with 2 tablespoons maple sugar

1. Puree rice with ricemilk, tofu, rice syrup, maple syrup, spices, dissolved kuzu or arrowroot and vanilla in a food processor. Pour the rice puree into a baking dish; mix in raisins and sunflower seeds and bake for 1 hour. Remove the pudding from the oven; sprinkle with cinnamon-sugar; and bake 10 minutes longer.

2. Serve pudding warm or at room temperature, plain or with maple cider sauce, nuts or fruit. Rice pudding firms as it cools.

GOOD BAKER'S TIPS & VARIATIONS
Although the rice is pureed, it retains some texture so the pudding is chewy.
Serve individual rice puddings: Ladle rice pudding into lightly oiled ramekins.
Place ramekins on a sheet pan. Bake puddings for 30 minutes.
Serve topped with warm ricemilk and fresh or dried fruit and/or nuts.

MAPLE CIDER SAUCE

1 - 1/3 CUPS

Good with pancakes, rice puddings, baked apples, this less sweet alternative to maple syrup is less expensive too. Serve warm.

GETTING STARTED
Small pot

INGREDIENTS
1 cup apple cider
2 to 4 tablespoons maple syrup
1 tablespoon freshly squeezed lemon juice
1/2 teaspoon ground cinnamon
2 teaspoons kuzu or 4 teaspoons arrowroot dissolved in 1 tablespoon apple cider

1. Put apple cider, maple syrup, lemon juice and cinnamon into the pot and simmer for 10 minutes. Add dissolved kuzu or arrowroot starch, stirring constantly. Cook kuzu 1 to 2 minutes after the boil; cook arrowroot only to the boil. Cool slightly before serving.

GOOD BAKER'S TIPS & VARIATIONS
If the sauce is too thick, add more cider.
Maple cider sauce will stay fresh up to 3 days. Store it in a jar in the refrigerator.
Raisins and nuts are nice additions to the sauce.

Chapter 3

Cookies & Bars

small bites...big taste

Crisp cookies-soft cookies-thin ones & bars
The aroma of fresh baked cookies.......
one of life's nicest little pleasures.

Make some Great Good Cookies Naturally

Watch the cookie monster smile.

Healthy Desserts 101
stop dying for a cookie and make some Great Good Cookies Naturally.

Cookies seem to be a universal comfort food. They are easy to make. The hardest part is trying not to eat too many. The word cookie comes from the Dutch word koekje, which means little cake. In fact, bar cookies such as brownies, are made from a cake-like batter. Cookies generally contain less liquid than cakes and are formed individually. Batter is either dropped from a spoon or shaped by hand. Cookies bake in a relatively short time. Be careful not to over bake them.

>> Most cookies can be baked ahead and stored in tightly covered jars.
>> Make sure cookies are completely cool before they are stored.
>> Basic cookie batter is easily varied, as are baked cookies.
   Roll or press raw cookie dough in chopped nuts or dry unsweetened coconut before it is baked. Stir chips, nuts and seeds into the batter.
>> Sandwich two baked cookies together with a filling of jam, melted chocolate, cream or icing.

BAKING PANS   SHEET PANS   COOKIE SHEETS   JELLYROLL PANS

What is the difference? Does it matter? A pan that is rimless on at least one side but usually on more than one side is called a cookie sheet. A pan with shallow rims on all four sides is known variously as a baking sheet, sheet pan or jellyroll pan. Buy a few heavy pans in the largest size that will fit into your oven and bake cookies.

Baking sheets are the most versatile pans. Use this type of pan to bake thin sheet cakes, keep nuts, seeds, oats and granola from spilling during handling and to contain any spillover from juicy fruit pies.

Cookies can be baked on shallow sided baking pans but rimless cookie sheets allow better air circulation so cookies bake more evenly. If you are baking more than 1 pan of cookies at a time, reverse the pans, front to back, and upper and lower racks halfway through baking.

Cookies bake most evenly on shiny, light colored aluminum cookie sheets and stainless steel pans. Aluminum cookie sheets conduct heat better than stainless steel. Lining the sheet pan with parchment paper protects the dough from the aluminum and creates a non-stick sheet pan.

Dark pans hold bottom heat making these pans terrific for baking pies which need strong bottom heat to quickly set the crusts, but they are bad for cookies. The bottoms of cookies baked on dark pans are often too dark or burned.

The Recipes

BASIC WHEAT FREE COOKIE

ORANGE GINGER CRISPS

OATMEAL RAISIN COOKIES

HONEY-FREE SAVE THE BEES BAKLAVA

CAROB FUDGE BROWNIES

DOUBLE CHOCOLATE FUDGE BROWNIES

FRANKLY AMAZING LOW-FAT CHOCOLATE BROWNIE

A GOOD PAN OF CORNBREAD

PEANUT BUTTER PUFFED CEREAL TREATS

CRUNCHY CARAMEL POPCORN TREATS

GOOD GOURMET GORP

PEANUT BUTTER CHOCOLATE CANDY CUPS

Basic Wheat-Free Cookies

24 TO 28 COOKIES

These delicious cookies, also called jam dots, are adapted from a recipe by Richard Pierce, master vegan chef and director of NYC's Whole Foods Project. The basic recipe is easily varied, see tips.

GETTING STARTED
Preheated 350-degree oven
Two cookie sheets lined with parchment paper
Wire cooling rack

INGREDIENTS
1 cup rolled oats, roasted and cooled
1 cup almonds or other nuts, roasted and cooled
1/2 cup rice flour
1/4 teaspoon sea salt
1 teaspoon ground cinnamon
1/2 teaspoon ground mace or nutmeg
2 tablespoons canola oil
3 tablespoons maple syrup
3 tablespoons apple juice
1 teaspoon apple cider vinegar
2 teaspoons vanilla extract
1 teaspoon almond extract
Optional:
1/4 cup unsweetened coconut
Chopped nuts, Currants

1. Grind oats in food processor. Add nuts and process until the mixture is finely ground. Pour the mixture into a bowl, add rice flour, salt and spices and stir with a spoon.

2. In a small bowl mix the wet ingredients: oil, maple syrup, apple juice, vinegar and extracts with a wire whisk until foamy.

3. Pour the wet ingredients into dry ingredients and mix well. A piece of dough should hold together when squeezed in your hand. Form walnut-size balls of dough; flatten each piece on a parchment-lined cookie sheet. Form an indentation in the center of each cookie with your finger. Fill the indentations with a small amount of all-fruit jam and bake 10 to 12 minutes until cookies are lightly browned. Alternatively, bake the cookies unfilled. Cool and fill with jam, chocolate or carob frosting.

GOOD BAKER'S TIPS & VARIATIONS
1/4 cup rice syrup can replace the maple syrup-apple juice mixture.
REPLACE THE RICE FLOUR with 5 tablespoons barley flour plus 3 tablespoons cornmeal.
CHOCOLATE CHIP COOKIES: Add 1/3 cup non-dairy chips, chocolate or carob, to the batter.
COCO-NUTS: Flatten pieces of dough. Press unsweetened coconut and chopped nuts into them before baking.
SANDWICH COOKIES: Spread jam or chocolate frosting on a baked cookie and top with another. Dip one side of the sandwich into melted chocolate, chill until chocolate has hardened

ORANGE GINGER CRISPS

3 DOZEN SMALL / 1 DOZEN LARGE COOKIES

I like thin, crisp cookies and as dairy-free versions are hard to find, I created these spicy gems, now favorites of my students and clients. If you prefer milder cookies, reduce the ginger powder to 3/4 teaspoon. The batter contains no chemical leavening, baking powder or baking soda so it can be made up to 24 hours before baking. Store cookies in a tin or tightly covered jar for 5 days or freeze for up to 1 month.

GETTING STARTED
 Preheated 325-degree oven
 Two cookie sheets lined with parchment paper
 Wire cooling rack

INGREDIENTS
 1/4 cup whole wheat pastry flour
 1/4 cup unbleached white flour
 2 tablespoons arrowroot
 1/4 teaspoon sea salt
 1 1/2 teaspoons ground ginger
 1/4 teaspoon ground mace
 Pinch of ground mustard
 2 tablespoons canola oil
 2 tablespoons orange juice
 1/4 cup rice syrup, warmed
 1/4 cup maple syrup
 1 teaspoon orange extract
 1/4 teaspoon vanilla extract

1. Sift dry ingredients: flours, arrowroot, salt and spices into a medium bowl. Stir with a wire whisk to mix.

2. In another bowl, mix wet ingredients: oil, orange juice, rice and maple syrups and extracts until thick. Pour the wet ingredients into dry ingredients and mix until batter is smooth. The consistency will resemble pancake batter. Refrigerate batter 1 hour or longer prior to baking cookies.

3. Stir batter and drop by teaspoons or tablespoons onto lined cookie sheets leaving 2 inches between cookies. These cookies really spread. Bake cookies until the edges are lightly golden brown, 13 to 15 minutes, then remove from oven.

TUILES. Immediately pick up each cookie with a spatula and drape or bend over a rolling pin or bottle until cool. They do not release easily from the paper. The cookies might harden before they are shaped. In that case, warm them in a 250-degree oven for a few minutes, they will soften.
FLAT COOKIES. Slide cookies, still attached to parchment paper onto a cooling rack. Cool 5 minutes; lift the cookies from the parchment paper with a spatula. Cooled cookies are crisp and release easily.
COOKIE CUPS. Drape a warm cookie over the bottom of a small cup or jar, turned upside down, until they harden. This takes only a few minutes. Fill cookie cups with pudding or mousse or non-dairy frozen dessert.

 OATMEAL RAISIN COOKIES

17 SMALL COOKIES / 8 LARGE COOKIES

We can't have a cookie chapter without oatmeal raisin cookies, but we can make them without butter, eggs and refined sugar. This recipe makes chewy, not gummy cookies. Don't over bake or the cookies will be dry. Make any size cookie you like but maintain a uniform thickness. Store cooled cookies in tightly covered containers.

GETTING STARTED
Preheated 350 degree oven
Cookie sheet lined with parchment paper
Wire cooling rack

INGREDIENTS
1/4 cup currants or raisins
1/4 cup orange juice
1/2 cup oat flour
3/4 cup whole wheat pastry flour
1/2 teaspoon baking powder
1/4 teaspoon baking soda
1 teaspoon ground cinnamon
1/2 teaspoon sea salt
1 cup rolled oats
2 tablespoons + 1 teaspoon canola oil
1/3 cup maple syrup
1 tablespoon barley malt
1 tablespoon vanilla extract
1 teaspoon apple cider vinegar

1. Cover the raisins with orange juice and set aside to soften for 10 minutes.

2. Mix the dry ingredients: flours, oats, baking powder, baking soda, salt and cinnamon in a medium bowl. Stir with a wire whisk to mix.

3. Drain the raisins, saving the juice for another use. Mix the wet ingredients: oil, maple syrup, barley malt, vanilla and vinegar until well combined in a small bowl. Pour the wet ingredients into dry ingredients and mix until dough holds together. Cover and refrigerate the dough for 30 minutes or up to overnight.

4. Remove dough from refrigerator. Pinch off pieces of dough, roll in your hands into walnut size balls or use an oiled ice cream scoop (2 tablespoons) to measure portions. Flatten each cookie to about 1/4 inch, keep the thickness even. Bake 7 to 8 minutes. The cookies will be slightly puffed, the tops will be dry and the bottoms light brown.

5. Remove cookie sheet from the oven, slip a spatula under each cookie and gently lift cookies onto cooling rack. Hot cookies are fragile; they firm as they cool. Store cooled cookies in a tightly covered jar.

GOOD BAKER'S TIPS & VARIATIONS
Make fresh oat flour as it is needed. Grind toasted, cooled rolled oats in a blender.
It is easiest to shape the cookies with slightly wet hands.
Sprinkle maple or evaporated cane juice onto cookies before baking, stir in chopped nuts.

 HONEY-FREE SAVE THE BEES BAKLAVA

40 TO 50 PIECES

No, this one is not low fat, but the cloying sweetness of standard baklava is gone. My friend Elaine prefers the name Honey I Saved the Bees Baklava.

GETTING STARTED
Preheated 350 degree oven
Oiled 9 x 13-inch baking pan
Wire cooling rack
Defrost frozen phyllo, wrapped, in the refrigerator.

INGREDIENTS
SWEET SYRUP
1 1/4 cups water
1 1/4 cups rice syrup
1 cinnamon stick
Whole cloves
1 organic lemon, sliced
1/2 organic orange, sliced

BAKLAVA
1 pound roasted walnuts, cooled and finely chopped
1/4 cup ground cinnamon, divided
3/4 cup canola oil
1 pound of phyllo dough

1. Put all syrup ingredients into a large pot and cook to a boil. Reduce heat and simmer for 30 minutes. Strain the syrup and discard the spices and fruit. Sweet Syrup can be refrigerated up to 2 weeks.

2. Mix chopped nuts and 2 tablespoons of ground cinnamon in a medium bowl.

3. Mix canola oil with 2 tablespoons ground cinnamon in a small bowl to make cinnamon oil. You might not use all the cinnamon oil, refrigerate it for another use.

4. Open the package of phyllo and place it on a lightly dampened tea towel. Phyllo dries out in a flash. Keep the top covered as well. Cut the phyllo to fit the baking pan and start layering. Gently pick up 2 pieces of phyllo together and lay them in the baking dish. Brush the top sheet with cinnamon oil. Add another 2 sheets, brush the top sheet with cinnamon oil and continue layering, brushing every second sheet with cinnamon oil until 10 sheets of phyllo are in the pan. Cover the top sheet with half the nut mixture. Add 4 more sheets of phyllo, continuing to brush every other piece with cinnamon oil. Sprinkle the balance of the nut mixture on top and layer 10 more sheets of phyllo, using the same method. Make sure the top piece of phyllo is well coated with cinnamon oil.

5. With a sharp knife, cut baklava into squares of desired size, and then cut each square into two triangles. Make sure to cut all the way to the bottom. Bake baklava on center rack of the oven for 1 hour or until golden brown and puffy. Cool 30 minutes and pour hot syrup over the baklava.

CAROB FUDGE BROWNIES

8 TO 16 PIECES

These fudge brownies are rich, so small squares should satisfy. Wrap and store brownies in the freezer, they defrost quickly. Carob powder is also called carob flour.

GETTING STARTED
Preheated 350 degree oven
Oiled 9-inch square pan
Wire cooling rack

INGREDIENTS
1 1/4 cups whole wheat pastry flour
1/2 cup unbleached white flour
1/4 cup arrowroot
3/4 cup carob powder, roasted and cooled
1 1/2 teaspoons baking powder
1/4 teaspoon baking soda
1/4 teaspoon sea salt
1/2 teaspoon ground cinnamon
1/4 cup canola oil
1/4 cup vanilla soymilk
1/4 cup prune puree or apple butter (see recipe for prune puree below)
3/4 cup maple syrup
1 tablespoon vanilla extract
1/2 cup chopped almonds

1. Sift dry ingredients: flours, arrowroot, carob, baking powder, baking soda, salt and cinnamon into a medium bowl. Stir with a wire whisk to mix.

2. In another bowl or in a blender, mix wet ingredients: oil, soymilk, prune puree, maple syrup and vanilla until smooth.

3. Pour wet ingredients into dry ingredients, mix quickly but thoroughly and stir in nuts. Spread batter into prepared pan.

4. Bake brownies on center rack of oven, 22 to 25 minutes, or until surface looks puffed and dry. A skewer inserted into the center should have a few crumbs clinging. Do not over bake the brownies. Cool pan on wire rack and refrigerate before cutting into squares.

PRUNE PUREE
1 cup dried, pitted prunes
Boiling water to cover prunes by 1 inch.
Soak prunes in boiling water for 15 minutes.
Puree prunes in a blender with approximately 3/4 of the soaking liquid until smooth.

GOOD BAKER'S TIPS & VARIATIONS
After cutting brownies, spread with carob glaze and place one whole nut on each piece. Refrigerate to set glaze.

DOUBLE CHOCOLATE FUDGE BROWNIES

8 TO 16 PIECES

Another good brownie, this one is a little richer. For triple chocolate fudge brownies, frost with Ultimate Chocolate Frosting, page 78. I got an e-mail from Doug in Philadelphia who followed this recipe. He wrote, "I'm no baker but these brownies = Nirvana." I hope you'll agree.

GETTING STARTED
    Preheated 350 degree oven
    Oiled 8-inch square baking pan
    Wire cooling rack

INGREDIENTS
    1 1/2 cups whole wheat pastry flour
    3/4 cup Dutch process cocoa
    1 1/4 teaspoons baking powder
    1/4 teaspoon baking soda
    1/4 teaspoon sea salt
    1/2 cup canola oil
    3/4 cup maple syrup
    1/4 cup barley malt
    1/4 cup water
    1 teaspoon vanilla extract
    1/2 teaspoon almond extract
    1/3 cup refined-sugar free chocolate chips

1. Sift dry ingredients: flour, cocoa, baking powder, baking soda and salt into a medium bowl. Stir with a wire whisk to mix.

2. In another bowl or in a blender, mix the wet ingredients: oil, maple syrup, barley malt, water and extracts until thoroughly combined. Pour wet ingredients into dry ingredients, and mix quickly but thoroughly, stir in chips. Spread batter in the prepared pan and smooth top. Bake brownies until top looks dry, 15 to 16 minutes. Place the pan on a cooling rack. When the pan of brownies is cool, cover with plastic and refrigerate or freeze before cutting.

GOOD BAKER'S TIPS & VARIATIONS
Replace chips with 1/2 cup toasted chopped walnuts.

THE BROWNIE SUNDAE
A SPECIAL VERY ONCE IN A WHILE TREAT.
FROST A BROWNIE WITH CHOCOLATE ICING.
ADD A SCOOP OF CHOCOLATE SORBET.
DRIZZLE WITH CHOCOLATE SAUCE.
EAT EXTRA GREENS TOMORROW

Frankly Amazing Low-Fat Chocolate Brownies

8 TO 16 PIECES

Unencumbered by nuts, these are brownies for chocolate lovers. Made with tofu, fruit puree and only 2 tablespoons of oil, they are frankly amazing. Eat one straight from the freezer; the taste is ultra-fudge.

GETTING STARTED
    Preheated 350 degree oven
    Oiled 9-inch square baking pan
    Wire cooling rack

INGREDIENTS
    1 1/4 cups whole wheat pastry flour
    1/4 cup arrowroot
    3/4 cup Dutch process cocoa
    1/4 cup maple sugar
    1/2 teaspoon baking powder
    1/4 teaspoon baking soda
    1/2 teaspoon sea salt
    1/2 teaspoon ground cinnamon
    1/4 cup blanched and pressed tofu
    2 tablespoons canola oil
    1 cup maple syrup
    1/2 cup prune puree (page 56) or apple butter
    2 teaspoons vanilla extract
    1/2 cup dairy-free, refined-sugar free chocolate chips

1. Sift dry ingredients into a medium bowl: flour, arrowroot, cocoa, maple sugar, baking powder, baking soda, salt and cinnamon. Stir with a wire whisk to mix.

2. Puree tofu with oil in a blender. Add maple syrup, prune puree and vanilla and blend again until smooth.

3. Pour the wet ingredients into dry ingredients and mix until batter is smooth. Stir in chocolate chips. Spread the batter into the prepared pan and smooth the top. Bake brownies on center rack of oven 20 to 23 minutes or until the surface looks dry. A cake tester inserted into the center removes almost, but not completely, crumb-free. Do not over bake or the brownies will be cake-like or too dry.

4. Place the pan on a wire rack. When the pan of brownies is cool, cover with plastic and refrigerate or freeze before cutting into squares.

A PAN OF GOOD CORNBREAD

9 X 9 SQUARE PAN

Cornbread! It is not just for BBQs anymore. I enjoy this cornbread for breakfast and snacks. The batter makes good muffins and when thinned with a little soymilk, makes cornmeal pancakes. I have served this cornbread to Southerners who thought it tasted just like home. They were stunned to learn the cornbread was low fat and made without dairy or eggs. By the way, I have learned over time to let the food speak for itself, rather than announce—eggs-dairy-sugar-free. That often sets up an expectation of yuck.

GETTING STARTED
Preheated 425 degree oven
Oiled 9 x 9-inch baking dish
Wire cooling rack

INGREDIENTS
1 cup cornmeal
1/2 cup whole wheat pastry flour
1/2 cup unbleached white flour
1 tablespoon + 1 1/2 teaspoons baking powder
1/4 teaspoon sea salt
1/2 cup + 2 tablespoons vanilla soymilk
1/2 cup filtered water
3 tablespoons maple syrup
2 tablespoons canola oil
2 teaspoons vanilla extract
Optional: 1/2 cup corn kernels
Maple syrup or jam for glazing and serving

1. Sift the dry ingredients into a medium bowl: cornmeal, flours, baking powder and salt. Stir with a wire whisk to mix.

2. In another bowl, mix the wet ingredients: soymilk, water, maple syrup, canola and vanilla with a wire whisk until foamy. Pour the wet ingredients into dry ingredients. Mix quickly but thoroughly with a wire whisk until batter is smooth. The batter will quickly thicken; it should fall off a spoon like heavy pancake batter.

3. Pour the batter into prepared pan, smooth the top and bake until cornbread is lightly browned, 15 to 18 minutes.

4. Cool cornbread, in the pan, on a wire rack for 10 minutes before cutting. Brush cornbread with maple syrup or jam, if you wish.

GOOD BAKER'S TIPS & VARIATIONS
BUY FRESH, WHOLE-CORN MEAL and store it in the refrigerator or freezer to prevent the oils in the germ from becoming rancid. This recipe is as fast to make and bake as any mix and has none of the junk contained in boxed mixes, refined, enriched cornmeal, sugar and salt.

MUFFINS: Fill oiled cupcake tins with batter, bake 15 to 20 minutes at 400 degrees. Make cornsticks using a cornstick pan, of course.

SKILLET CORNBREAD: Oil a cast iron pan and heat it in the oven before adding the batter. The cornbread will be crusty on the sides and bottom. Toast cornbread or brush with some maple syrup, if the cornbread becomes dry. Stir 1 cup of blueberries, corn kernels, sautéed bell pepper or onions into the batter.

PEANUT BUTTER PUFFED CEREAL TREATS

16 TO 32 PIECES

Here is a wheat and maple-free candy for both younger kids and older kids to enjoy. Organic PB and good chips, chocolate or carob, plus dried fruit, seeds and nuts create a no-bake, healthful snack reminiscent of rice crispy treats. Vary the nut butter, nuts, dried fruit, even the cereal to create other versions. It is important to purchase peanuts and peanut products from reputable, organic growers. Peanuts are susceptible to aflotoxin, a mold that is thought to be carcinogenic.

GETTING STARTED
Line an 8 x 8-inch square pan with plastic wrap and parchment paper.
Medium heavy-bottom pot

INGREDIENTS
1/2 cup rice syrup
2 tablespoons peanut butter, smooth or crunchy
1 tablespoon cocoa or carob powder
1 1/2 cups puffed rice cereal
1 cup peanuts, lightly toasted
1/3 cup toasted sesame seeds
1 cup currants or raisins
1 cup non-dairy chocolate or carob chips

1. Pour rice syrup into the pot and warm it over low heat. Stir peanut butter and cocoa into the syrup and simmer, stirring until the mixture is smooth. Be very careful, syrups tend to climb the sides of the pot when they are heated, creating a messy and dangerous situation.

2. Combine cereal, nuts, currants and chips in a large bowl. Carefully pour the warm syrup over all and stir with a wooden spoon until coated.

3. Press the still warm mixture into the prepared pan. A piece of parchment on top makes this easy to do. Cover the pan with plastic wrap and refrigerate. When the Peanut Butter Cereal Treats are firm, 30 minutes to 1 hour, cut them into squares or bars and store in an airtight tin.

GOOD BAKER'S TIPS & VARIATIONS
Roll the mixture into balls and wrap individually.

CRUNCHY CARAMEL POPCORN TREATS

ABOUT 6 CUPS

Do you remember looking for the prize in the box of caramel corn? Surprise! That nutritional nightmare, white sugar, corn syrup, molasses, saturated fat and salt was the booby prize. Our updated version made with low-calorie, high fiber popcorn, features rice syrup and barley malt standing in for the refined sugars. Make some and watch a movie.

GETTING STARTED
Preheated 350 degree oven
Medium pot
Baking sheet lined with parchment paper

INGREDIENTS
1/4 cup plus 2 tablespoons rice syrup
1/4 cup barley malt
1/2 teaspoon sea salt
1 teaspoon apple cider vinegar
2 tablespoons water
1 tablespoon cashew butter
1 teaspoon vanilla extract
1/2 teaspoon almond extract
6 cups unsalted, air popped popcorn
1/2 cup sunflower seeds, toasted

1. In a medium saucepan, over low heat, slowly cook rice syrup, barley malt, salt and cider vinegar to a low boil. Reduce heat and immediately stir in water and cashew butter. Simmer uncovered, until the mixture is smooth, 4 to 5 minutes. Be very careful; syrups are extremely hot. Remove the pot from the stove and add extracts.

2. Mix popcorn with sunflower seeds in a large bowl. Carefully pour hot syrup over all. Mix until popcorn and seeds are coated with syrup. Transfer to lined baking sheet and bake in upper third of oven for 6 to 7 minutes, stirring once, or until golden brown and almost, but not completely dry. When the treats have cooled, transfer them to an airtight container and store at room temperature.

GOOD BAKER'S TIPS & VARIATIONS
The cider vinegar adds a caramel note to the sweeteners.
The cashew butter can be eliminated if nut allergies are an issue.

GOOD GOURMET GORP

ABOUT 5 CUPS

GORP, GOOD OLD RAISINS & PEANUTS, *has been through rehab. Still, all you need to make this version is a bowl, a spoon, sugar-free, low-fat granola, homemade or purchased, nuts and dried fruit. Avoid brightly colored (sulfite treated), sugar-added, dried fruit. Use any nut you like but change the name.*

GETTING STARTED
Preheated 375-degree oven
Oiled 1 1/2 quart baking dish
Food processor

INGREDIENTS
2 cups sugar-free granola
3/4 cup roasted peanuts
1/2 cup dried apples
1/2 cup raisins or currants
1/2 cup chopped dates
1/3 cup dried apricots

1. Mix all ingredients together in a bowl.

2. Store GORP refrigerated in a covered jar. Enjoy plain, or sprinkled on soy yogurt, jells and puddings.

PEANUT BUTTER & CHOCOLATE CANDY CUPS

30 MINI CUPS

I practically lived on PB Cup candies one semester at college. I don't know why, but I do know this wasn't a good thing. Tofu and organic peanut butter, both healthful foods, are the main players in this cleaned up version, but it's still not okay to eat too many.

GETTING STARTED
 Small pot
 Food processor or blender, small, clean paintbrush or offset spatula
 Miniature foil baking cups
 Parchment lined baking sheet or flat tray

INGREDIENTS
 Filtered water
 1/4 of a 1 pound box of firm tofu, blanched and pressed
 1/4 teaspoon sea salt
 1/4 cup maple syrup
 3 tablespoons organic peanut butter
 3 tablespoons maple sugar
 3 tablespoons Dutch process cocoa
 1 teaspoon pure vanilla extract
 3/4 teaspoon almond extract
 2 tablespoons filtered water
 1 cup dairy-free bittersweet chocolate chips
 1 teaspoon canola oil

1. Cream the tofu in a food processor or blender with salt and maple syrup. Add peanut butter, maple sugar, cocoa and extracts and blend again until very creamy. Add water if necessary to achieve a consistency that resembles heavy pancake batter. Spoon the mixture into a container. Cover and refrigerate for one hour.

2. Chocolate cups: Line a baking pan with plastic wrap and a piece of parchment paper. Put chocolate into a small heatproof bowl over a pot of simmering water and stir until the chocolate is melted and smooth. Do not overheat chocolate. Remove the bowl from the pot and dry the bottom. Use a small paintbrush or offset spatula, to coat the inside of each paper cup with melted chocolate. Put finished cups on the baking pan. Use your fingers to wipe off any chocolate that may get onto the outside of the cups; keep wet and dry towels at hand. Put the tray of chocolates into the freezer. When the chocolate has hardened, add a second coat and freeze again.

3. Peel the paper off the chocolate when it is hard. If the chocolate softens, freeze. Store chocolate cups in a covered container for up to 1 month. To assemble candy cups, see page 64.

GOOD BAKER'S TIPS & VARIATIONS
Chocolate can be melted in a heatproof bowl in a 225-degree oven or in a double boiler. It is important that not even a drop of water come in contact with the melted chocolate or it will seize (harden). It is difficult, actually impossible, to fix chocolate that has seized. It turns grainy and dull. Spread the peanut butter cream in a baked tart shell. Spread with melted chocolate and sprinkle with chopped nuts to make a knockout peanut butter cream pie.

PEANUT BUTTER & CHOCOLATE CANDY CUPS

ASSEMBLE THE CANDY CUPS

Spoon the cream filling into the chocolate cups. Alternatively, use a pastry bag fitted with a fluted tip, to pipe cream into cups. The cream-filled cups can be prepared up to a week ahead. Place the cups in a container, separate layers with parchment paper, cover tightly and freeze until needed.

CHOCOLATE COATED LEAVES

Learn to make the candy cups and you will know how to make chocolate leaves.

Place chocolate leaves on a finished cake or a tray of fancy cookies for a knockout presentation. I garnish dessert plates with one chocolate large leaf; they are stunning. This is a labor intensive project, but the leaves, like the candy cups can be made in advance and stored in a covered container in the refrigerator.

1. Select pesticide-free, pliable leaves that have prominent veins, such as lemon, camellia or rose. Use a pastry brush to cover the underside (the veined side) of each leaf with melted chocolate; wipe off any chocolate that goes over the edge.

2. Put the chocolate-coated leaves on a parchment covered baking sheet and refrigerate until the chocolate hardens. Carefully peel the leaves away from the hardened chocolate. If the chocolate starts to melt, return the leaves to the refrigerator or freezer.

NOTE: SOME PLANTS ARE POISONOUS. MAKE SURE YOU CHOOSE SAFE LEAVES.

NOTES

Chapter 4

Great Good Cakes

layer cakes & plain cakes
special occasion & just because

Yes! We can have our birthday cakes and eat them too!

Healthy Desserts 101
Cakes

Honestly, I think these recipes make the best and easiest homemade cakes ever.
They just happen to be good for you. It is easy to learn to make 'for goodness cakes'.

SECRETS TO GREAT TASTING GOOD CAKES
Fresh good quality ingredients - Accurate measurements - A calibrated oven - A relaxed baker - The correct size pan

Remember to read the entire recipe before you begin and be sure you understand the

information. Gather all ingredients, prepare them and preheat and check the

temperature of your oven. If your oven is set to 350-degrees but the thermometer

reads 375-degrees, re-set the oven to 325-degrees

Use a pastry brush to oil the pans prior to baking. I don't dust the pans with flour, but I do line them with parchment paper. This guarantees cakes that release easily every time.

Baking times are only guidelines but do not open the oven door to peek at the cakes before the minimum time has elapsed. If you do, the center of the cake might collapse. You might be able to cut the center out and call it a bundt cake.

A layer cake is simply alternating layers of cake, usually two, but sometimes more, filling and frosting. I prefer the term cake design to cake decorating. Simple looks best, but do have fun with presentation. Cold cakes are easier to slice into layers fill and frost. Pair cakes with complementary sauces and creams but remember that sometimes a slice of plain cake tastes just right.

Tightly wrapped unfrosted cake layers can be frozen up to a month. Defrost cakes, still wrapped in the refrigerator. Condensation will stay on the wrapping and off the cake.

Cakes can be moistened with maple cake wash, the healthy alternative to sugar syrup. Mix 1/4 cup maple syrup, 2 tablespoons water and 1/2 teaspoon vanilla extract in a small jar. Maple cake wash replaces simple syrup, which is sugar syrup that is used in bakeshops to flavor and moisten cakes. Store cake wash in the refrigerator for up to 2 weeks.

SERVING SIZES ARE OF COURSE APPROXIMATE.
8 to 9-inch layer cake   10 to 12 portions
10 to12-inch layer cake   14 to 16 portions
9 x 9-inch pan   8 to 16 portions

TO CUT AN 8 OR 9-INCH SQUARE PAN OF BROWNIES, FOR EXAMPLE INTO PORTIONS,
Cut the cake into quarters. Cut each quarter in half. You now have 8 pieces.
Cut in half again to makes 16 pieces.

The Recipes

THE VERSATILE VANILLA CAKE

BASIC TOFU CREAM FROSTING

TROPICAL FRUIT GATEAU

LEMON-LIME TOFU CREAM

LOVELY LIGHT LEMON CAKE

LUSCIOUS LEMONY TOFU CREAM

THE CHOCOLATE CAKE TO LIVE FOR

CHOCOLATE TOFU CREAM

ULTIMATE CHOCOLATE SAUCE

ULTIMATE CHOCOLATE FROSTING

LEMON GLAZED 24 KARAT CAKE

DREAMY LEMON CREAM

CAROB CAKE

CAROB ICING

BETTER BOSTON CREAM PIE

CUSTARD CREAM FILLING

CAROB GLAZE

UNCOFFEE CAKE

PEANUT BUTTER & JELLY POWER MUFFINS

MAPLE GLAZED CRANBERRIES

THE VERSATILE VANILLA CAKE

10 TO 12 SERVINGS

Learn the technique used to make this vanilla cake and you'll have the foundation recipe for many different desserts. Choose any icing or tofu cream to fill and frost your cake. Alternatively, spread the cake with all-fruit jam, or simply serve with fresh fruit. Serving a single layer cake, sometimes called a torte, is an elegant and delcious way to cut the per serving calories and fat.

GETTING STARTED
Preheated 350 degree oven
Two 8-inch cake pans, oiled and bottoms lined with parchment paper
Wire cooling racks

INGREDIENTS
1 cup plus 2 tablespoons whole-wheat pastry flour
3/4 cup plus 2 tablespoons unbleached white flour
1 1/2 teaspoons baking powder
1/2 teaspoon baking soda
1/2 teaspoon sea salt
1/4 cup canola oil
3/4 cup plus 2 tablespoons maple syrup
3/4 cup vanilla ricemilk or soymilk
2 teaspoons apple cider vinegar
3 tablespoons vanilla extract

1. Sift the dry ingredients into a medium bowl: whole-wheat pastry flour, unbleached white flour, baking powder, baking soda and sea salt. Stir with a wire whisk to mix.

2. In another bowl, mix the wet ingredients, canola oil, maple syrup, soymilk, vinegar and vanilla, with a wire whisk until foamy. Pour the wet ingredients into dry ingredients and mix until the batter is smooth.

3. Pour the batter into the pans dividing evenly. Level the tops by gently rotating pans. Tap the pans lightly on the counter to eliminate air bubbles. Bake cakes on center rack of the preheated oven 20 to 25 minutes, or until the cake is golden brown and springs back at its center when touched lightly. A cake tester inserted in the center of the cake should remove clean.

4. Remove cakes from the oven and place the pans on cooling racks. Allow the cakes to cool in the pans for 10 minutes, then use a dinner knife to release the layers from the sides of the pan. Turn layers out of pans, directly onto wire racks to finish cooling.

5. When cool, enclose each layer tightly in plastic wrap. Refrigerate until layers are cold, about 1 hour, before filling and frosting, or over wrap in aluminum foil. Freeze for longer storage.

GOOD BAKER'S TIPS & VARIATIONS
Leftover or stale cake can be toasted and made into crumbs. Store cake crumbs in a bag in the freezer. Sprinkle crumbs on top of cakes or press into the frosting on the sides. A sprinkling of cake crumb adds nice texture and taste to fruit salads, puddings and jells. One half cup of chopped dried fruit, chocolate or carob chips, nuts or dried coconut can be mixed into the batter. Make cupcakes with the batter. Do not use paper liners with dairy-free batters.

 Basic Tofu Cream Frosting

4 CUPS

This is the tofu cream to use for cake decorating. Agar and kuzu or arrowroot add stability to the cream. Now you can play with your pastry tips and bags. You will need to rewhip the cream, which is meant to be very firm. Remember the drill! Organic tofu is best. Always blanch and press tofu prior to using it for reliable results.

GETTING STARTED
Small pot
Food processor
Vegetable juice for tinting cream (see tips)

INGREDIENTS
1 pound firm tofu, blanched and pressed
1/2 cup maple syrup
2 tablespoons lemon juice
1/2 teaspoon sea salt
1 tablespoon vanilla extract
1 teaspoon almond extract
2 tablespoons smooth cashew or almond butter or canola oil
1/2 cup fruit-sweetened juice such as lemonade, apple juice or water
3 tablespoons agar flakes
3/4 cup vanilla soymilk
3 tablespoons kuzu or 6 tablespoons arrowroot, dissolved in 5 tablespoons juice or water
Optional: 1/4 to 1/2 cup maple sugar

1. Process the tofu with maple syrup, lemon juice, salt and extracts in a food processor until it is creamy, 2 to 3 minutes. Add nut butter and process 1 minute longer, or until tofu is very smooth.

2. Pour juice into a medium pot and sprinkle agar flakes onto surface of juice. Do not stir or heat and allow agar to soften for 10 minutes.

3. Cover the pot and over medium heat, bring agar and juice to a low boil. Reduce heat and simmer about 5 minutes to dissolve the agar. Stir in soymilk and simmer 2 to 3 minutes longer.

4. Whisk the dissolved kuzu or arrowroot into the dissolved agar stirring constantly and cook over low heat until the mixture is thick (it will be very thick, this is OK). Be careful not to scorch the bottom of the pot. Spoon the mixture into the creamed tofu, process until smooth. Taste and add sweetener and color as desired. Refrigerate cream at least 1 hour or up to 24 hours. The tofu cream will be very firm. Two hours before you plan to use the frosting, cream it in a food processor and chill it again for 30 minutes to 1 hour.

GOOD BAKER'S TIPS & VARIATIONS
Tint tofu creams with highly colored vegetable and fruit juices.
Red-Beet Juice (it is very strong; mix it in drop by drop) >> Green-Parsley Juice >>Yellow-tumeric dissolved in a little vanilla extract and water >> Orange-Carrot juice- Purple >> Mix blueberry and raspberry juices to make purple.

 TROPICAL FRUIT GATEAU

10 TO 12 SERVINGS

A moist, orange layer cake dolled up with citrus tofu cream and tropical fruit becomes a gateau. Make a fabulous orange cake (double the recipe for 2 layers) and spread with orange marmalade or add chips to the batter and fill and frost with chocolate or carob frosting.

GETTING STARTED
Preheated 350 degree oven
One 9-inch round cake pan, oiled and bottom lined with parchment paper
Wire cooling rack
Suggestion: One recipe Lemon-Lime Tofu Cream (page73)

INGREDIENTS:
3/4 cup whole wheat pastry flour
3/4 cup unbleached white flour
3/4 cup plus 1 tablespoon maple sugar
1/2 teaspoon baking powder
1 teaspoon baking soda
1/2 teaspoon sea salt
1 cup orange juice
1/4 cup plus 1 tablespoon canola oil
1 tablespoon maple syrup
1 tablespoon apple cider vinegar
1 teaspoon vanilla extract
1/2 teaspoon orange extract
2 tablespoons grated orange zest
Fruit suggestions: 2 kiwis / mango / berries
1/2 cup fruit sweetened jam: orange marmalade or berry all fruit jam
Optional: 1/3 cup dried unsweetened coconut

1. Sift the dry ingredients into a medium bowl: flours, maple sugar, baking powder, baking soda and salt. Stir with a wire whisk to mix.

2. In another bowl mix the wet ingredients, orange juice, oil, maple syrup, vinegar and extracts, with a wire whisk until foamy, stir in orange zest. Pour the wet ingredients into dry ingredients. Use a wire whisk to mix quickly but thoroughly until batter is smooth.

3. Pour batter into the cake pan and level the top. Bake the cake on center rack of a preheated oven for 25-30 minutes or until cake is lightly golden and springs back at its center when touched lightly. A cake tester inserted into the center of cake removes clean.

4. Cool pan on wire rack about 10 minutes. Run a dinner knife around the sides of the pan, carefully releasing cake. Turn layer out of pan directly onto wire rack. Cool completely, wrap cake tightly in plastic wrap and refrigerate before cutting the layer into 2 thin layers (torte the cake).

5. Chop kiwis, mango and large berries into small pieces. Heat the jam in a small pot, add fruit and stir gently to glaze fruit. Set aside until time to assemble torte.

LEMON-LIME TOFU CREAM

2 1/2 TO 3 CUPS

This tart, fresh tasting tofu cream pairs beautifully with the Tropical Fruit Gateau.
While this is a soft tofu cream, it does firm somewhat during chilling.

GETTING STARTED
Food processor

INGREDIENTS
1 pound firm silken tofu
1/3 cup smooth cashew butter
1/4 cup maple syrup
1/4 to 1/3 cup maple sugar
1/2 teaspoon sea salt
3 tablespoons lemon juice
2 tablespoons lime juice
1 teaspoon vanilla extract
1 teaspoon lemon extract
2 tablespoons grated zest (lemon and lime)

1. Cream the tofu in a food processor, stopping the machine a few times to scrape the sides. Add cashew butter, maple syrup, maple sugar, salt, lemon and lime juice and extracts. Continue processing until cream is very smooth. Add zest and pulse once or twice.

2. Spoon the cream into a container, cover and refrigerate for at least 4 hours to allow flavors to blend and the cream to thicken.

TO ASSEMBLE THE TROPICAL FRUIT GATEAU
Use a serrated knife to cut the cake horizontally into 2 thin layers. It is easier to divide a cake into layers (torte the cake) when it is elevated. A cake-decorating turntable is handy, but not essential. Bend down to eye level with the cake, mark the outside by cutting into the cake a little, then slowly cut all the way through. Use a cake cardboard circle or rimless cookie sheet to lift off the top layer. Don't worry if the layers aren't perfectly even. Put bottom layer, cut side up, on a serving plate and spread with half the tofu cream. Cover cream with half the glazed fruit. Place second layer on filling and press down lightly. Spread with lemon-lime tofu cream; arrange sliced fruit decoratively on top and sprinkle with optional coconut. Refrigerate cake at least 30 minutes before slicing. Serve any leftover fruit with the cake.

GOOD BAKER'S TIPS & VARIATIONS
The brightly colored skin of citrus fruit is the zest. The white covering just under the zest is called the pith and is bitter. It is economical to zest organic citrus fruit before juicing the fruit. Zest can be frozen tightly wrapped.

 LOVELY LIGHT LEMON CAKE

10 TO 12 SERVINGS

Lemony, moist and tender, this maple syrup sweetened cake is filled and iced with Luscious Lemony Tofu Cream. For a stunning holiday cake, spread Maple Glazed Cranberries over the cream. This cake is a favorite of my friend, vegan baker extraordinaire, Francis James of Seattle.

GETTING STARTED
    Preheated 350 degree oven
    Two 8-inch cake pans, oiled and bottoms lined with parchment paper
    Wire cooling racks
    Suggestion: One recipe Luscious Lemony Tofu Cream (page 75)
    One recipe Maple Glazed Cranberries (page-89)

INGREDIENTS
    1 cup whole wheat pastry flour
    1 cup unbleached white flour
    1 1/2 teaspoons baking powder
    1 teaspoon baking soda
    1/2 teaspoon sea salt
    1 tablespoon grated lemon zest
    1/3 cup canola oil
    3/4 cup maple syrup
    1/3 cup vanilla soymilk or ricemilk
    1/3 cup water
    1/4 cup plus 2 tablespoons lemon juice
    2 teaspoons apple cider vinegar
    1 teaspoon vanilla extract
    2 teaspoons lemon extract
    Garnish: 1/4 cup dried unsweetened coconut

1. Sift dry ingredients into a large bowl: flours, baking powder, baking soda and salt. Add lemon zest. Stir with a wire whisk to mix.

2. In another bowl mix the wet ingredients, oil, maple syrup, soymilk, water, lemon juice, vinegar and extracts with wire whisk until foamy. Pour the wet ingredients into dry ingredients and mix quickly but thoroughly until batter is smooth.

3. Pour the batter into prepared cake pans, dividing evenly. Bake on center rack of preheated oven for 25 to 30 minutes or until cake is lightly browned and springs back at center when lightly touched. A cake tester inserted into the center of the cake removes clean. Place cake pans on wire racks to cool for 10 minutes. Use a dinner knife to carefully release cakes from the sides of the pan. Turn layers out of pans directly onto wire racks; cool completely. Wrap each layer tightly in plastic wrap and refrigerate 1 hour before icing the layers, or over wrap in aluminum foil and freeze.

GOOD BAKER'S TIPS & VARIATIONS
Freshly squeezed citrus juice is always best but organic lemon and lime juices are now available in some markets. Make a Lemon Poppy Seed Cake. Add 1/3 cup toasted poppy seeds to the batter and bake per recipe. Brush cake with warm apricot jam.

 Luscious Lemony Tofu Cream

1 1/2 CUPS

I am crazy about this cream; it tastes of fresh lemon juice. If nut allergies are a consideration, replace the cashew butter with 2 tablespoons of canola oil. The turmeric adds a yellow tint.

GETTING STARTED
Food processor

INGREDIENTS
Pinch of turmeric
1 tablespoon lemon juice plus 1/4 cup
1 pound firm tofu, blanched and pressed
3 tablespoons smooth cashew butter
1/2 cup maple sugar
1/2 teaspoon sea salt
Grated zest of 1 lemon (about 2 tablespoons)
1 1/2 teaspoons vanilla extract
1 1/4 teaspoons lemon extract

1. Dissolve turmeric in 1 tablespoon of lemon juice.

2. Crumble tofu into bowl of food processor, add cashew butter and process for 5 minutes. Stop the processor and scrape down sides of the bowl. Add maple sugar, salt and 1/4 cup lemon juice and continue to process until tofu is smooth and creamy. Add lemon zest, extracts and dissolved turmeric, blend 30 seconds longer. Spoon the cream into a container, cover and refrigerate for at 3 hours to allow flavors to blend and cream to thicken.

TO ASSEMBLE THE CAKE
Place bottom layer on serving plate and spread with one-third to one-half the lemon cream. Place top layer on filling, press down lightly. Spread the balance of the tofu cream on top with. Spoon a layer of maple glazed cranberries over the cream. Refrigerate cake at least 40 minutes or up to overnight before serving. Serve at room temperature.

THE CHOCOLATE CAKE TO LIVE FOR

10 TO 12 SERVINGS

The botanical name for chocolate, Theobroma cacao, means food of the gods. This tender chocolate cake filled and frosted with rich tasting chocolate cream, perhaps drizzled with shiny chocolate glaze more than lives up to that name. I am regularly told, "This can't be healthy, it tastes like a real chocolate cake". My answer, "It is both."

GETTING STARTED
Preheated 350 degree oven
Two 9-inch round cake pans oiled and bottoms lined with parchment paper
Wire cooling racks
Suggestion: Chocolate Tofu Cream (page 77) -Ultimate Chocolate Frosting (page79)

INGREDIENTS
1 cup whole wheat pastry flour
1 cup unbleached white flour
2 teaspoons baking powder
2 teaspoons baking soda
1 teaspoon sea salt
1/2 teaspoon cinnamon powder
1/2 cup plus 2 tablespoons Dutch process cocoa
1/2 cup maple sugar
1/2 cup canola oil
1 cup maple syrup
1 cup vanilla soymilk
1 cup water
2 teaspoons balsamic or apple cider vinegar
1 tablespoon vanilla extract
1/2 teaspoon almond extract

1. Sift dry ingredients into a large bowl: flours, baking powder, baking soda, salt, cinnamon, cocoa and maple sugar. Stir with a wire whisk to mix.

2. In another bowl, mix the wet ingredients with a wire whisk until foamy: oil, maple syrup, soymilk, water, vinegar and extracts.

3. Pour the wet ingredients into dry ingredients and mix gently but thoroughly until the batter is smooth. Don't panic; this batter is very thin. Pour batter into pans, dividing evenly. Bake on center rack of preheated oven for 25 to 30 minutes or until center of cake springs back when lightly touched and a cake tester inserted into center of cake removes clean.

4. Cool cake layers in pans on wire cooling racks for 10 minutes. Use a dinner knife to release cakes from sides of pans. Turn layers out of pans directly onto racks, cool completely. Wrap layers tightly in plastic wrap and refrigerate before assembling the cake.

GOOD BAKER'S TIPS & VARIATIONS
Dutch process cocoa can be replaced by natural cocoa; an additional 1/2 teaspoon of baking soda is needed. The taste is slightly different, some tasters think it's deeper. Why not make both variations and see which you prefer.

 CHOCOLATE TOFU CREAM

2 1/2 CUPS

The color and texture of this tofu cream reminds me of milk chocolate butter cream. I like this cream better and hope you will too. For a deeper chocolate flavor, add Ultimate Chocolate Glaze (page 78) to taste to the cream.

GETTING STARTED
Food processor

INGREDIENTS
1 pound firm tofu, blanched and pressed
2 tablespoons canola oil
1/4 teaspoon sea salt
1/3 cup Dutch process cocoa
1/4 cup maple sugar
2 to 4 tablespoons maple syrup
2 teaspoons vanilla extract
1/2 teaspoon almond extract

1. Process tofu with oil and salt in a food processor. Add cocoa, maple syrup and extracts. Process until smooth and creamy. This might take as long as 5 minutes. Add maple sugar or cocoa to taste. Spoon cream into a container, cover and refrigerate at least 2 hours and up to 24 hours to allow flavors to blend and cream to firm.

TO ASSEMBLE THE CAKE

COCOA CREAM CAKE
Place strips of waxed paper around the edge of a serving plate. Put one layer on the plate, spread with one-third of the chocolate tofu cream. Cover with the second layer, press down lightly. Frost sides and top of cake with the remaining tofu cream. Chill the cake for at least 1 hour or up to overnight. Remove waxed paper before serving. Drizzle the cake with chocolate glaze or sauce.

DARK CHOCOLATE CAKE
Fill and frost cake with Ultimate Chocolate Frosting.

COMBO CAKE
Fill with Chocolate Tofu Cream and frost with Ultimate Chocolate Frosting.

ULTIMATE CHOCOLATE SAUCE

1 1/2 CUPS

Keep a jar of this versatile, delicious, easily made, virtually fat-free sauce in your refrigerator and chocolate treats are moments away. Use this sauce to make hot cocoa, milk-free-shakes, smoothies, chocolate icing and more.

GETTING STARTED
Food processor

INGREDIENTS
3/4 cup Dutch process cocoa
1/2 cup maple sugar
1/4 teaspoon sea salt
1/2 cup boiling water
1/2 cup maple syrup
1 tablespoon vanilla extract

1. Put cocoa, maple sugar and salt into a food processor and pulse to combine. With the motor running, pour boiling water through the feed tube. Stop the processor, scrape down the sides and add maple syrup and vanilla. Process again until smooth. The sauce will be thin; it thickens when it is cold. Pour the sauce into a storage jar and refrigerate for at least 4 hours or up to 1 week.

GOOD BAKER'S TIPS & VARIATIONS
To make chocolate glaze:
Reduce the water to 1/4 cup and add 1 tablespoon of smooth almond or cashew butter.

ULTIMATE CHOCOLATE FROSTING

1 1/2 CUPS (ENOUGH FOR AN 8 OR 9-INCH CAKE)

This is my favorite chocolate frosting. It is virtually fat-free and an absolute pleasure to spread. The frosting is tofu and nut-free, thus suitable for folks with allergies. Most importantly, it tastes great. An overnight rest in the refrigerator brings this frosting to the right consistency; additional thickener is not necessary. I prefer to make the frosting a day in advance. John Borders, Louisville's gourmet vegan chef, cake-decorator and all around wonderful man, wrote: "Fran, YOU NAILED IT! A very low-fat frosting that tastes great and spreads like a dream."

GETTING STARTED
    Medium pot with heavy bottom
    One recipe: Ultimate Chocolate Sauce (page 78) warm or at room temperature

INGREDIENTS
    1 1/2 cups Ultimate Chocolate Sauce, warm or at room temperature
    2 tablespoons kuzu or 1/4 cup arrowroot, dissolved in 3 tablespoons water

1. Pour the chocolate sauce into a pot and over very low heat bring the sauce to just under a boil. Add dissolved kuzu or arrowroot to hot sauce, stirring rapidly. Cook kuzu 1 to 2 minutes after the boil, arrowroot just to the boil. Lift the pot on and off the heat as a precaution against scorching when the frosting starts to bubble and thicken. Pour frosting into a container, cool to room temperature, cover and refrigerate 2 hours to overnight. It may need even longer chilling before the consistency is just right but it gets there.

GOOD BAKERS TIPS & VARIATIONS
Have patience when cooking the frosting; it must be allowed to heat slowly, like an egg-based custard.

A large number of non-dairy frostings depend on nut butter or soy margarine for richness and "spreadability" and many are tofu based. Since I don't use hydrogenated fats, soy margarine was not an option. Still, I wanted to create a frosting that tasted rich, spread like butter cream and was suitable for those with nut and or soy allergies. I hope you will agree that this fits the bill.

LEMON GLAZED 24 KARAT CAKE

8 TO 10 SERVINGS

This crown jewel of carrot cakes is moist, light and spiced just right. This is not an old-fashioned, heavy, oil-laden cake, in fact, it is a frequently requested wedding cake. A food processor makes fast work of grating carrots but a hand grater is fine too. Toast a slice of plain cake for a nice change of pace. Don't be put off by the long ingredient list, this is an easy cake to make.

GETTING STARTED
> Preheated 350 degree oven
> Wire cooling racks
> Two 8-inch cake pans oiled and bottoms lined with parchment paper
> Suggestion: One recipe of Dreamy Lemon Cream (page 81)

INGREDIENTS

1/2 cup raisins	1/2 teaspoon ground cloves
1/3 cup orange juice	1/4 cup canola oil
1 cup whole wheat pastry flour	1 cup plus 2 tablespoons maple syrup
1 cup unbleached white flour	1/2 cup vanilla soymilk
1 teaspoon baking powder	2 tablespoons orange juice, reserved from raisins
1 teaspoon baking soda	1 1/2 teaspoons orange extract
1/2 teaspoon sea salt	1/2 teaspoon vanilla extract
2 teaspoons cinnamon powder	2 cups peeled, shredded carrots, packed
1/2 teaspoon ground mace or nutmeg	

GARNISH: 1/2 CUP CHOPPED NUTS, UNSWEETENED COCONUT , 8 TO 10 WHOLE NUTS

1. Put raisins into a small bowl, cover with orange juice and set aside to plump for 5 to 10 minutes. Drain the raisins, reserving the juice.

2. Sift dry ingredients into a large bowl: flours, baking powder, baking soda, salt and spices. Stir with a wire whisk to mix.

3. In another bowl, mix the wet ingredients, oil, maple syrup, soymilk, orange juice and extracts, with a wire whisk until foamy.

4. Pour the wet ingredients into dry ingredients and mix until batter is smooth. Stir grated carrots and drained raisins into the batter with a rubber spatula. Spread batter into the prepared cake pans dividing evenly and smooth the tops. Bake cakes on center rack of the preheated oven for 30 to 35 minutes or until cakes are golden brown and spring back at their center when touched lightly. A cake tester inserted in the center of cake, removes clean.

5. Place cake pans on wire racks to cool 10 minutes, then use a dinner knife to release cake from sides of pan. Turn layers out of pans onto wire racks; cool completely. Wrap each layer tightly in plastic wrap and refrigerate before assembling the cake.

DREAMY LEMON CREAM

2 1/2 CUPS

A beautifully balanced versatile lemon cream that looks and tastes similar to lemon curd – but without egg yolks and butter. Spread a baked tart shell with a thin layer of Lemon Cream, pile high with seasonal peaches, plums, cherries or berries and serve a French style pastry jewel. Sugar-free organic lemonade is available in health food stores and many supermarkets.

GETTING STARTED
Medium pot
Food processor

INGREDIENTS
1 1/3 cups plus 1/4 cup natural lemonade (fruit sweetened, divided)
2 tablespoons agar flakes
1/2 teaspoon sea salt
1/2 cup maple syrup
1/2 cup ricemilk
3 pinches turmeric (for color)
1 tablespoon kuzu or 2 tablespoons arrowroot, dissolved in 1/4 cup fruit juice
1 teaspoon lemon extract
1/2 teaspoon vanilla extract
1/3 cup lemon juice
1 tablespoon minced lemon zest

1. Pour lemonade into a medium pot and sprinkle agar flakes on juice. Don't stir or heat and allow agar to soften for 10 minutes. Add salt.

2. Cover the pot and over medium heat bring juice and agar to a boil. Uncover, reduce heat and simmer until agar is completely dissolved, stirring occasionally for 5 to 10 minutes. Continue to simmer until agar has completely melted into the juice.

3. Add turmeric, maple syrup and ricemilk to the pot. Add dissolved kuzu or arrowroot to hot sauce, stirring rapidly. Cook kuzu 1 to 2 minutes after the boil, arrowroot just to the boil. Remove pot from the stove and stir in extracts, lemon juice and zest.

4. Pour the cream into a shallow dish and cool uncovered for 10 minutes. Cover surface of cream with plastic wrap, poke a few holes with a sharp knife and refrigerate cream until it is set. If cream becomes too stiff to spread, cream it in a food processor.

TO ASSEMBLE THE CAKE
Place one layer on a serving plate, spread with one-third the Dreamy Lemon Cream and top with second layer. Press down lightly and spread top of cake with enough cream to cover. Sprinkle outside border of cake with chopped nuts and coconut and mark each serving with one perfect nut.

GOOD BAKER'S TIPS & VARIATIONS
Dreamy lemon cream can be refrigerated up to 3 days.

CAROB CAKE

10 TO 12 SERVINGS

The recipe for this cake is based on the recipe for the best carob cake ever, Jenny Matthau's carob walnut cake. Jenny is co-director of the Natural Gourmet Cookery School in New York City.

GETTING STARTED
Preheated 350 degree oven
Two 9-inch round cake pans oiled/ bottoms lined with parchment paper
Wire cooling racks
Suggestion: 1 recipe Carob Icing, (page 83)

INGREDIENTS
3/4 cup whole wheat pastry flour
3/4 cup unbleached white flour
3 tablespoons plus 1 teaspoon carob powder
2 teaspoons baking powder
1/4 teaspoon baking soda
1/2 teaspoon sea salt
1/2 teaspoon cardamom powder (see tips)
1/4 cup canola oil
3/4 cup plus 2 tablespoons maple syrup
2 tablespoons barley malt
1/2 cup vanilla soymilk
1/4 cup water
1 1/2 teaspoons apple cider vinegar
1 1/2 teaspoons vanilla extract
Optional: 1/3 cup chopped nuts

1. Sift all dry ingredients into a large bowl: flours, carob, baking powder, baking soda, salt and cardamom. Stir with a wire whisk to mix.

2. In another bowl, mix the wet ingredients, oil, maple syrup, barley malt, soymilk, water, vinegar and vanilla with a wire whisk until foamy. Pour wet ingredients into dry ingredients and mix until batter is smooth. Mix in optional chopped nuts.

3. Pour the batter into the pans, dividing evenly, and smooth the tops. Bake cakes on center rack of the preheated oven 25 to 30 minutes, or until the cake has risen, looks dry and springs back at its center when touched lightly. A cake tester inserted in the center of cake removes clean.

4. Place cake pans on wire racks to cool for 10 minutes. Use a dinner knife to carefully release layers from sides of pan. Turn layers out of pans directly onto wire racks and cool completely. Wrap each layer tightly in plastic wrap and refrigerate to chill before icing the layers, or over wrap in aluminum foil and freeze for longer storage.

GOOD BAKER'S TIPS & VARIATIONS
Cardamom powder compliments the flavor of carob, but it is not essential. If you do not have any, make the cake anyway.

CAROB ICING

1 1/3 CUP

A dark, shiny, good icing. Carob can be gritty; cook long enough to ensure the icing is smooth.

GETTING STARTED
   Medium pot

INGREDIENTS
   1/2 cup maple syrup
   1 tablespoon barley malt
   1/2 cup water (more to adjust consistency)
   1/2 teaspoon sea salt
   1 cup carob powder, roasted and cooled
   1/4 teaspoon cardamom powder
   1/2 teaspoon cinnamon powder
   1 tablespoon grain coffee substitute
   2 tablespoons cashew butter
   1 tablespoon canola oil
   1 tablespoon vanilla extract
   1 teaspoon almond extract
   Optional: chopped fruit and nuts for filling

1. Pour maple syrup and barley malt into a pot and cook to a low boil over medium heat. Reduce heat to low; stir in 1/2 cup water and salt. Whisk in carob powder and cook 10 minutes.

2. Add cardamom, cinnamon, grain coffee, nut butter and oil. Simmer, stirring occasionally for 10 minutes or until the icing is smooth and shiny. Add water if the icing is too thick.

3. Remove the pot from the stove; stir in extracts. Cool icing to lukewarm; it spreads more easily when slightly warm.

GOOD BAKER'S TIPS & VARIATIONS
The addition of thinned carob icing or glaze to basic tofu cream makes a good cake filling.

TO ASSEMBLE THE CAROB CAKE
Put one cake layer on serving plate and spread with a layer of icing. Top with optional chopped fruit or nuts. Cover with second layer and press down lightly. Spread top of cake with balance of icing and sprinkle with nuts if desired. Chill cake briefly before slicing.

BETTER BOSTON CREAM PIE

8 TO 10 SERVINGS

Fill tender cake layers with non-dairy custard, pour shiny carob or chocolate glaze over the top and a traditional American cake is successfully updated. Why might a cake be called a pie? Food historians say pie plates were more common in the kitchens of early settlers and that may be the answer. The original Boston Cream Pie recipe calls for sponge cake filled with pastry cream and topped with chocolate butter icing. The cholesterol is history; the flavor remains.

GETTING STARTED
Preheated 350 degree oven
Two 8-inch round cake pans, oiled/bottoms lined with parchment paper
Wire cooling rack
Suggestion: 1 recipe of Carob Glaze (page 86) or Ultimate Chocolate Frosting (page79)

INGREDIENTS
1 cup whole wheat pastry flour
1 cup unbleached white flour
1 teaspoon baking powder
1 teaspoon baking soda
1/2 teaspoon sea salt
1/4 cup canola oil
3/4 cup maple syrup
1/3 cup soymilk
1/4 cup water
3 tablespoons orange juice
2 teaspoons apple cider vinegar
2 teaspoons vanilla extract
1 teaspoon orange extract

1. Sift dry ingredients into a large bowl: flours, baking powder, baking soda and salt. Stir with a wire whisk to mix.

2. In a smaller bowl, mix the wet ingredients: oil, maple syrup, soymilk, water, orange juice, vinegar and extracts. Beat with a wire whisk until foamy. Pour the wet ingredients into dry ingredients and mix quickly but thoroughly until the batter is smooth.

3. Pour the batter into the pans, dividing evenly. Level the tops by gently rotating pans. Bake cakes on center rack of preheated oven 20 to 30 minutes or until cake is golden brown and springs back at its center when touched lightly. A cake tester inserted into the center of the cake removes clean.

4. Place pans on wire racks to cool 10 minutes. Use a dinner knife to release cakes from the sides of the pans. Turn layers out directly onto wire racks; cool completely. Wrap each layer tightly in plastic wrap and refrigerate until cakes are cold.

CUSTARD CREAM FILLING

1 1/4 CUP

Agar and kuzu or arrowroot replace the eggs in traditional custard. Add a tiny pinch of turmeric for an "eggy" color if you wish.

GETTING STARTED
Medium pot with cover

INGREDIENTS
1/2 cup sugar-free lemonade or water
1 1/2 tablespoons agar flakes
1 cup vanilla soymilk
3 tablespoons maple syrup
3 tablespoons maple sugar
1/4 teaspoon sea salt
1 1/2 tablespoons kuzu or 3 tablespoons arrowroot, dissolved in 2 1/2 tablespoons water
1 tablespoon vanilla extract
1 teaspoon almond extract
Pinch of turmeric dissolved in as little water as possible

1. Pour the lemonade into a medium pot and sprinkle agar flakes onto surface of juice. Do not stir or heat and allow agar to soften for 10 minutes. Cover the pot and over medium heat bring juice and agar to a boil. Uncover, reduce heat and simmer until agar is completely dissolved, stirring occasionally, for 5 to 10 minutes. Add soymilk, maple syrup and salt and simmer 2 to 3 minutes longer.

2. Add dissolved starch (kuzu or arrowroot) to the pot, stirring constantly, and cook over low heat until the mixture boils. Reduce heat and cook 1 minute longer if using kuzu; cook arrowroot only until a boil is reached.

3. Remove pot from the stove and stir in extracts. Pour custard into a shallow bowl, cool and cover the dish. Refrigerate the custard until it is set. Stir custard vigorously with a spoon before it is used.

GOOD BAKER'S TIPS & VARIATIONS
Add two to four tablespoons of cashew butter or Silken Nut Cream (page 39) for a richer custard.

CAROB GLAZE

1 1/2 CUP

This glaze is dark, shiny and good. Make sure to cook the glaze long enough to eliminate any trace of graininess.

GETTING STARTED
Medium pot

INGREDIENTS
1 cup carob powder, roasted and sifted
1 1/3 cups maple syrup
2 tablespoons barley malt
1/2 cup orange or other fruit juice
1/2 cup all fruit jam
1 teaspoon sea salt
1 teaspoon cardamom powder
1 teaspoon cinnamon powder
4 teaspoons kuzu or 2 tablespoons plus 2 teaspoons arrowroot, dissolved in 2 tablespoons water
2 tablespoons vanilla extract
1 teaspoon almond extract

1. Put carob into a medium pot. Stir in maple syrup, barley malt, 1/2 cup juice or water, jam, salt, cardamom and cinnamon. Simmer mixture, stirring occasionally, for 10 minutes or until glaze is shiny and smooth. Add dissolved starch (kuzu or arrowroot) to the pot, stirring constantly, and cook over low heat until the mixture boils. Reduce heat and cook 1 to 2 minutes longer if using kuzu; cook arrowroot only to a boil. Remove pot from the stove and stir in extracts. Cool glaze and refrigerate up to 1 week. Adjust consistency with additional water or other liquid if glaze becomes too thick to spread.

TO ASSEMBLE THE BOSTON CREAM PIE
Warm glaze in a water bath: put a heatproof jar, filled with glaze, into a pot of simmering water to keep the glaze warm.

Place one cake layer bottom side up on a flat plate, spread with custard, cover with second layer and press down lightly. Cover the cake with plastic wrap and refrigerate for 1 hour or up to overnight. Remove cake from the refrigerator. Pour warmed glaze over the top allowing some glaze to drip down the sides. Refrigerate assembled cake, unwrapped for at least 45 minutes until glaze is set.

GOOD BAKER'S TIPS & VARIATIONS
The method for roasting carob is found on page 23.
If the glaze does not taste perfectly smooth, add one tablespoon oil or nut butter and simmer longer..

UNCOFFEE CAKE

12 OR MORE SERVINGS

This became my signature cake at Angelica Kitchen. It's a big cake, nutty, moist and fragrant with spice. Enjoy a slice with a steaming cup of your favorite beverage. Sprinkle the filling on other batters. Cupcake Uncoffeecakes?

GETTING STARTED
    Preheated 350 degree oven
    One 9-inch springform pan, oiled/bottom lined with parchment paper
    Wire cooling rack

INGREDIENTS FILLING
    1 3/4 cups walnuts, roasted, cooled, coarsely chopped
    1/2 cup maple sugar
    2 teaspoons cinnamon powder
    3 tablespoons canola oil

1. Mix walnuts, maple sugar and cinnamon in a small bowl. Stir in oil and mix until filling is moist; set aside while you make the cake batter.

INGREDIENTS CAKE
    1 cup whole wheat pastry flour
    1 cup unbleached white flour
    3 tablespoons maple sugar
    1 teaspoon baking powder
    1 teaspoon baking soda
    1/2 teaspoon sea salt
    2 teaspoons cinnamon powder
    1/4 teaspoon ground cloves
    1/4 teaspoon ground nutmeg, mace or allspice
    1/4 cup canola oil
    3/4 cup plus 2 tablespoons maple syrup
    3/4 cup vanilla soymilk or ricemilk
    1 tablespoon apple cider vinegar
    2 tablespoons vanilla extract

1. Sift dry ingredients into a medium bowl: flours, maple sugar, baking powder, baking soda, salt and spices and stir with a wire whisk.

2. In another bowl, mix wet ingredients, oil, maple syrup, soy or ricemilk, vinegar and vanilla. Beat with a wire whisk until foamy. Pour the wet ingredients into dry ingredients and mix until batter is smooth.

3. Pour 1/2 the batter into the oiled cake pan and sprinkle with 1/2 the filling. Pour the remaining batter over the filling and cover with the balance of filling. This is a big cake; the pan will be 3/4 full.

4. Bake the cake on center rack of preheated oven 50 to 55 minutes or until cake is golden brown. A cake tester inserted into the center of the cake removes clean. Cool cake in pan on a wire rack for 10 minutes, remove sides of pan and allow cake to cool completely.

 Peanut butter & Jelly Power Muffins

12 MUFFINS

Feel good, not guilty, when you grab a moist, power-packed, chock-full of healthful ingredients muffin. Vary the nut butter and jam as you like, but be sure to use very ripe bananas and room temperature peanut butter.

GETTING STARTED
    Preheated 375 degree oven
    Greased muffin tin

INGREDIENTS
    1 1/4 cups whole wheat pastry flour
    2 1/2 teaspoons baking powder
    1/2 teaspoon baking soda
    1/4 teaspoon sea salt
    3 tablespoons maple sugar
    1 teaspoon cinnamon powder
    1/3 cup plus 1 tablespoon rolled oats
    1/3 cup raisins
    1/3 cup peanuts, divided
    1 cup vanilla soymilk
    2 tablespoons canola oil
    1/3 cup maple syrup
    1 teaspoon vanilla extract
    1 tablespoon apple cider vinegar
    1 ripe banana, mashed with a fork, about 1/3 cup
    1/4 cup all-fruit jam, divided
    1/4 cup natural peanut butter

1. Sift the dry ingredients into a medium bowl: flour, baking powder, baking soda, salt and cinnamon. Stir with a wire whisk. Mix in oats, raisins and 1/4 cup of the peanuts.

2. Mix the wet ingredients in a medium bowl until blended.: soymilk, canola oil, maple syrup, vanilla extract, vinegar and mashed banana Pour the wet ingredients into the dry ingredients and mix only until the batter is smooth. Scoop a scant 1/3 cup batter per muffin into a cupcake tin, filling each cup to 3/4 of capacity. Quickly drop 1/4 teaspoon of jam and 2-3 peanuts on the center of each cupcake.

3. Bake muffins on center rack of preheated oven 25-28 minutes or until golden brown and a cake tester inserted into center of cake removes clean. Cool cupcakes in the pan on a wire rack for 10 minutes. Remove the cupcakes from the pan directly onto the rack; cool completely.

GOOD BAKER'S TIPS & VARIATIONS
The muffins do not turn out right when the banana has been pureed in a blender or food processor. I am not certain but think the liquefied banana adds too much liquid to the batter.
Frost the muffins with peanut butter and jelly before serving.
Make muffins in advance and store them in the freezer in a covered container or tightly closed freezer bag for up to 1 month.

MAPLE GLAZED CRANBERRIES

1 CUP

Sweet, tart, ruby red cranberries and no sugar rush; this is a real good thing. When cranberries are in season, buy several bags to store in your freezer. The berries are meant to remain whole so the cooking time is short. Cook the cranberries longer; add some orange juice and you'll have made cranberry sauce.

GETTING STARTED

Heavy skillet, about 8-inches across

INGREDIENTS

1/4 cup maple syrup
Pinch sea salt
1 cup cranberries
1/2 teaspoon orange extract

1. Pour the maple syrup into the bottom of a small, heavy skillet, add salt and heat to boiling, taking care the syrup does not burn or boil over. Stir in cranberries and cook until they just begin to burst. Remove skillet from the stove and stir in extract.

2. Remove berries from juice with a slotted spoon before spooning onto cake; save the syrup. It is yummy.

NOTES

NOTES

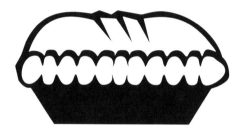

Chapter 5

Pies & Tarts

slumps & shortcakes

say goodbye to Fear of Flaking

Pies & Tarts
foolproof flaky pie dough everytime

Now repeat after me, I (state your name) can make a great pie crust!

Making pie dough actually takes less time than reading these notes.
Foolproofs are dairy-free crusts made with whole grain flours and
a neutral flavor vegetable oil such as canola or hi-oleic safflower oil.

The recipes include pies baked in pie plates
and freeform pies, also known as rustic pies and galettes.
Foolproof flaky pie dough can be used to make savory pies, such as pot pies.

The Mis En Place for Foolproof Flaky Pie Dough

Ice Cold Oil And Ice Water

Whole Wheat Pastry Flour

Unbleached White Flour

Sea Salt

Vinegar Or Lemon Juice

Parchment Paper For Rolling Dough

Heavy Baking Sheet Lined With Parchment

Heavy Rolling Pin

Hot Oven: 400 to 425 Degrees

Bake Pies On Lower Third Of Oven

The Recipes

ORIGINAL FOOLPROOF FLAKY PIE DOUGH

NEWEST FOOLPROOF FLAKY PIE DOUGH

THIS IS NOT MY MOTHER'S PUMPKIN PIE

FREEFORM APPLESAUCE GALETTE

STRAWBERRY RHUBARB-APPLESAUCE TART

FRESH STRAWBERRY SAUCE

FANCY SUMMER FRUIT TARTS

THREE GLAZES FOR TARTS

RUSTIC 3 BERRY PIE

BERRY CRISP IN A COOKIE PIECRUST

CHOCOLATE GLAZED STRAWBERRY SHORTCAKES

BLUEBERRY SLUMP

CRUMB TOPPING FOR COBBLERS AND FRUIT PIES

BAKED APPLE BISCUIT TOPPED COBBLER

CREAMY STRAWBERRY & DATE FILLING

HINT OF LEMON CUSTARD SAUCE

I promise piecrusts that are flaky, tender and easy as pie.

The secret to Foolproof Flaky Pie Dough is linking tried and true pie technique with natural ingredients.

The challenge to making flaky, tender, dairy-free piecrusts (that happen to be cholesterol-free) has been met. Typically, piecrusts are made with bleached white flour and solid vegetable shortening or butter and sometimes eggs.

The basic foolproof flaky non-dairy piecrust is made with whole-wheat pastry flour, unbleached white flour, ice-cold oil and ice water.

> Handle pie dough as little as possible.
> Use ice cold liquids and a little lemon juice or vinegar.
> Allow the dough to rest 2 times in the refrigerator.
> Bake pies in lower third of a hot oven.

Dairy-free pie dough is somewhat firmer than those made with solid fat. This is an advantage; no worries about soggy piecrusts, even after a day.

Healthy Desserts 101
how to make
foolproof flaky pie dough every time

Mix organic whole-wheat pastry flour with unbleached white flour in a 50/50 ratio. Pastry flour is softer and lower in protein than standard whole-wheat (bread) flour. Piecrusts made with all whole-wheat flour taste like cardboard and those made with only white flour are unpalatable (and unhealthful).

Mix lemon juice or vinegar into the ice water and drizzle slowly into the flour. Mix and toss with a rubber spatula, adding only enough water to form rough, soft dough. Turn the dough out of the bowl onto a large piece of plastic wrap, enclose the dough in the wrap, pat and press it to a round or oval disk. Refrigerate the dough for 30 minutes or up to 4 hours. This rest period allows the liquid to be absorbed, and allows any gluten that has developed to relax.

Roll the dough: Unwrap the dough and put it between two pieces of parchment paper. Using a heavy rolling pin, roll from the center out, turning the dough 45 degrees with each pass. Peel the paper off the dough after each complete turn. Refrigerate the dough if it softens or shrinks back. Continue rolling until the dough is 1/8 to 1/4-inch thick and about two to three inches larger than the pie plate.

Fit the dough into the oiled pie plate: Peel the top piece of parchment paper from the dough. Slip your hand under the parchment (and dough), lift and center dough over the oiled pie plate. Using the paper as a carrier, turn the dough over and ease it in. Don't stretch the dough or it will shrink during baking. Gently peel the paper from the surface of the dough. Trim excess dough with scissors, leaving a one-inch border for the pie (three-inches for freeform pies). Fold this dough towards the pie plate. Cover dough with plastic wrap and return it to the refrigerator for the second rest period. The edge can be finished just before the piecrust is filled.

'Baking blind' refers to baking a crust empty, that is, without a filling. Prick dough, bottom and sides with a fork. This is called docking. Cover dough with a sheet of crumpled parchment, weight with beans or pie weights and partially or fully bake. Do not fill until the crust is cool. The filling should be cool as well.

Pastry dough can be rolled out, wrapped and frozen for up to one week, but unrolled dough will not hold for more than four hours; the fat leaks out.

ORIGINAL FOOLPROOF FLAKY PIE DOUGH

DOUGH FOR ONE 9-INCH PIE OR 12-INCH FREEFORM GALETTE

This recipe was formerly named Perfect Vegan Pie Dough, but you do not have to be vegan to want to make (and eat) an easy, delicious piecrust.

GETTING STARTED
    Preheated 400 degree oven
    Parchment paper
    Rolling pin
    Pie plate or baking sheet
    Cooling rack

INGREDIENTS
    3/4 cup whole wheat pastry flour
    3/4 cup unbleached white flour
    1/2 teaspoon sea salt
    1/2 teaspoon cinnamon powder
    1/4 cup very cold canola oil (put a jar of oil in the freezer for 30 minutes)
    1 teaspoon lemon juice or apple cider vinegar
    1/4 to 1/3 cup ice water (add ice cubes to the water)

1. Sift flours, salt and cinnamon into a medium bowl. Stir with a wire whisk to mix and aerate.

2. Drizzle the cold oil over the flour, tossing and mixing with a rubber spatula until oil is coated with flour. Do not break up the irregular clumps that form. These clumps of fat are equivalent to the solid shortening in conventional piecrust and produce a flaky crust. Mix lemon juice or vinegar into 1/4-cup ice water and gently stir the liquid into the flour. Slowly add just enough additional water to form a rough dough. Transfer the dough onto a large piece of plastic wrap and enclose the dough. Press the dough package into a flat disk, round or oval depending upon your recipe. Refrigerate dough for 30 minutes or up to 4 hours.

3. Roll the dough: Unwrap the chilled dough and place between 2 large pieces of parchment paper. Roll from the center out; turn dough 45 degrees and repeat. After one full turn, carefully release the top paper, turn dough over, release the paper and repeat until dough is even and thin (1/8-1/4 inch thick), proper shape and size. If dough softens or shrinks back, chill.

4. If you are making a freeform, galette or rustic pie, leave the rolled dough in the parchment paper, cover with plastic wrap and refrigerate for 30 minutes or up to 4 hours. To fit the dough into the pie plate, carefully remove the top piece of parchment. Slip your hand underneath the parchment, lift and center it over the pie plate. Turn the parchment over and use it as a carrier to ease the dough in. Cover the surface of the dough with plastic wrap and refrigerate for at least 30 minutes before filling and baking.

GOOD BAKER'S TIPS & VARIATIONS

Make shapes such as leaves, stars, letters, from the dough using a sharp knife, or specialty cutters. Put the shapes on a cookie sheet and chill brefore baking. Brush the shapes lightly with maple syrup, barley malt and water (50-25-25) and bake at 400 degrees on a parchment lined cookie sheet until lightly brown and crisp. Arrange the baked designs decoratively on top of a baked pie. Both raw and baked dough can be stored in the freezer, in a covered container.

 Newest Foolproof Flaky Pie Dough

9-INCH CRUST

This version is made in exactly the same way as Original Foolproof. Here a small amount of sugar is added to the flour and soymilk is mixed into the water, creating a very tender piecrust. This dough is just slightly harder to handle. Make Original Foolproof Flaky Pie Dough a few times, then try this one and decide which you prefer.

GETTING STARTED
    Parchment paper
    Rolling pin
    Pie plate or baking sheet
    Cooling Rack

INGREDIENTS
    3/4 cup whole wheat pastry flour
    3/4 cup unbleached white flour
    3 tablespoons maple sugar
    1/4 teaspoon baking powder
    1/2 teaspoon sea salt
    1/4 cup very cold canola oil (put a jar of oil in the freezer for 30 minutes)
    1/4 cup ice water.
    3 tablespoons very cold vanilla soymilk
    1 teaspoon vanilla extract

1. Follow the recipe for Original Foolproof Flaky Pie dough.

2. Add 3 tablespoons maple sugar to the dry ingredients.

3. Mix 3 tablespoons very cold soymilk into the ice water.

THIS IS NOT MY MOTHER'S PUMPKIN PIE

8-INCH PIE

Presenting a holiday gift, zero cholesterol, creamy, full flavored pumpkin pie. Cover the baked pie with leaves baked from dough or cover with maple syrup glazed pecans. Replacing the pumpkin with squash or sweet potato works well. Sugar pumpkins make good pies but canned organic pumpkin is a reliable, convenient product. It is available in markets and by mail order, see resources list.

GETTING STARTED

    One recipe Foolproof Flaky Pie Dough
    Preheated 400 degree oven
    Parchment paper
    Rolling pin
    Oiled 8-inch pie plate
    Cooling rack

INGREDIENTS

    2 1/2 cups unsweetened pumpkin puree
    1 1/2 cups firm tofu, blanched and pressed
    1 teaspoon cinnamon powder
    1/4 teaspoon ground ginger
    1/4 teaspoon ground mace or nutmeg
    3/4 teaspoon sea salt
    3 tablespoons kuzu or 1/3 cup arrowroot powder, dissolved in 5 tablespoons orange juice
    1/2 cup maple syrup
    1/4 cup barley malt syrup
    1 teaspoon vanilla extract
    1/4 teaspoon lemon or orange extract

1. Puree pumpkin, tofu, spices and salt in a food processor. Add dissolved kuzu or arrowroot.

2. Add dissolved kuzu or arrowroot, maple syrup, barley malt and extracts. Process until filling is creamy and smooth. Spoon the filling into a bowl, cover and refrigerate 30 minutes or up to overnight.

3. Roll the dough between 2 pieces of parchment paper into a circle about 3 inches larger than the pie plate. Remove the parchment from the top of the dough. Lift the dough attached to the parchment, center it over the pie plate and ease it into the pie plate. Be sure not to stretch the dough or it will shrink during baking. Remove parchment. Trimming the dough is unnecessary, this is a rustic pie and the dough will be folded over the filling. Cover dough with plastic wrap and refrigerate 30 minutes to 4 hours.

4. Bake the pie: Take the dough from the refrigerator and unwrap. Spoon the filling into the pie shell mounding it higher in the center. Fold the sides of the dough up and over the filling. Bake pie in the bottom third of a 400 degree oven for 45 minutes. Remove the pie from the oven and brush the crust with maple syrup. Return the pie to the top third of the oven and bake 10 to 15 minutes longer, until filling is set and crust is golden brown. Cool the pie on a wire rack.

5. Cover the pie with plastic wrap and refrigerate. The filling will firm in 2 to 3 hours. The filling might crack as the pie cools; no problem. Warm the pie in a low oven before serving.

FREEFORM APPLESAUCE GALETTE

9 TO 10-INCH FREEFORM GALETTE

A jar of organic applesauce, some flours, cold oil and ice water, a hot oven and wow!
Homemade fast food and not so much as a pie plate to wash. Jacques Pepin, a well-known
chef and author defines a galette as a thin free-form tart. This galette meets the criteria.
It is hard to believe there is no butter.

GETTING STARTED

One recipe Foolproof Flaky Pie Dough
Preheated 400 degree oven
Parchment paper
Rolling pin
Baking sheet
Cooling rack

INGREDIENTS

3 to 4 cups unsweetened applesauce, homemade or purchased
1 or 2 apples
1 cup apple juice
1 teaspoon cinnamon powder stirred into 1/3 cup maple sugar
1/4 cup apricot or orange marmalade, warmed in small pot

1. Roll dough between 2 pieces of parchment, into an oval about 12 inches in diameter. Slip the baking sheet under the dough package and cover with plastic wrap. Refrigerate dough 30 minutes to 4 hours.

2. Peel, core and slice the apples thinly into a medium bowl and cover with apple juice. The juice prevents the apples from browning and, unlike lemon-water, adds taste.

3. Just before baking, peel the top sheet of parchment from the dough. Spread a layer of applesauce on the dough, leaving a 3 inch border uncovered. Use bottom piece of parchment to help fold dough up and over the applesauce. Bake the galette in the lower third of the oven for 40 minutes and remove.

4. Drain the apple, reserving the juice for another use and carefully arrange apple slices over the filling. Be careful, the baking sheet and pastry are hot. Sprinkle apples with maple sugar and cinnamon, and bake 10 to 15 minutes longer or until the apples are tender and the crust is golden brown.

5. Place galette, still on baking sheet, onto the cooling rack and brush crust with warmed jam. After 10 minutes, slide the galette, still on parchment paper, off the baking sheet onto the cooling rack to finish cooling.

6. The galette tastes best after a few hours at room temperature and it is perfectly fine the next day. Galettes can be warmed in 300-degree oven.

GOOD BAKER'S TIPS & VARIATIONS

Use this recipe as a template to create other freeform or rustic pies. Always leave a 2 to 3-inch border of dough to fold up around the filling. Taste the applesauce and add a few teaspoons of lemon juice, sweetener or cinnamon if you like, but time in the oven removes any taste of the jar.

STRAWBERRY RHUBARB-APPLESAUCE FREEFORM TART

9 TO 10-INCH FREEFORM GALETTE

The recipe for the applesauce galette on page 101 is the basic recipe for this fabulous rhubarb applesauce variation. Strawberries and rhubarb are natural partners. Try this tart with a topping of fresh strawberries.

GETTING STARTED

One recipe Foolproof Flaky Pie Dough, rolled to about 12 inches
Preheated 425 degree oven
Parchment paper
Rolling pin
Baking sheet
Cooling Rack

INGREDIENTS

3 cups unsweetened applesauce, homemade or purchased
1 cup sliced rhubarb
1/4 cup orange juice
1 cup sliced strawberries
1/4 cup strawberry or raspberry jam, warmed

1. Mix applesauce, rhubarb and orange juice together in a medium pot and cook on medium heat, stirring occasionally, until the rhubarb is soft, 10 to 15 minutes. If you like a chunky sauce remove the pot from the stove at this point. Continue to cook, stirring until the rhubarb has completely broken down if you prefer a smooth sauce. Cool the filling.

2. Spread a layer of rhubarb-applesauce on the dough, leaving a 3 inch border uncovered. Use parchment to help fold dough up and over the filling. Bake the tart on a parchment-lined baking sheet, in the lower third of the oven for 45 to 50 minutes, until the filling is bubbling and the crust is lightly browned. Remove from oven and cool on a rack.

3. Cover the filling with sliced strawberries and glaze with warm jam. Serve the tart with Fresh Strawberry Sauce, a cream or frozen non-dairy frozen dessert and a big sprig of mint.

GOOD BAKER'S TIPS & VARIATIONS
The leaves of the rhubarb plant are toxic.
The pink, celery-like stalks the edible part of the rhubarb plant.

FRESH STRAWBERRY SAUCE

1 1/2 CUP SAUCE

Berry sauces look beautiful and taste wonderfully fresh. Berries with many seeds, raspberries, for example, taste better when the sauce is pressed through a fine strainer.

GETTING STARTED
Food processor

INGREDIENTS
2 cups strawberries, washed and patted dry, divided
1 tablespoon maple sugar
1 teaspoon lemon juice
2 tablespoons orange juice
1 teaspoon mirin or a liqueur such as Chambord, Framboise, Grand Marnier
2 tablespoons seedless red berry all-fruit jam
1 to 2 teaspoons grated orange or lemon zest

1. Cut the strawberries in half or quarters, depending on the size. Put 1 1/2 cup of berries into a bowl. Mix in the sugar, lemon and orange juice, mirin or liqueur and jam, stirring to coat the berries. Set aside for 20 to 30 minutes to overnight. The berries will release liquid during this time.

2. Puree berries and any accumulated juice in a food processor. Stir zest and reserved 1/2 cup berries into the sauce.

CAUTION: It is important to try to find a source for fresh organic berries or purchase frozen, organic berries, such as those marketed by Cascadian Farms. Toxic chemicals are sprayed on conventionally grown berries and strawberries in particular are heavily sprayed. Because berries are soft and porous, it seems logical that a quick rinse, all you really can do with berries, may be futile.

The Secret to Making Fancy Summer Fruit Tarts.....
Even the ones with the French names are easy to make!

Entire books have been written about fruit tarts, detailed recipes abound, but the truth is that Tarte aux Fruit Rouges et Bleu is nothing more than a baked tart shell, spread with cream and filled with raspberries, strawberries and blueberries. And guess what, yours truly made up the name. A tart is composed of only a few elements, all of which are found within the pages of this book. Here is how to make plain and fancy fruit tarts.

Bake a cookie tart crust in a tart pan with a removable bottom. See recipe on page 108.

Cool. Brush the bottom with melted jam or chocolate.

Fill with Tofu Cream, Pudding, Mousse etc.

FANCY FRUIT TART VERSION 1
1. Arrange sliced fruit in concentric circles starting at the outside edge, overlapping the pieces slightly. Use different fruits for different circles if you like (think banana and mango, kiwi or sliced berries). Brush the fruit with melted jam to glaze. Chill up to 4, maybe 5 hours, but plan to serve the tart the same day.

2. If you prefer a more modern, less constructed look, forget the circles and arrange fruit in any way that pleases your eye. Stand some whole berries or pieces of fruit upright in the cream. Glaze fruit with melted jam.

FANCY FRUIT TART VERSION 2
1. Mix berries and diced fruit such as peaches, nectarines or a combination. Add toasted chopped nuts into a tofu cream, custard, pudding, date cream, etc. Lemon and lime flavored creams pair exceptionally well with summer fruit. Refer to the recipe lists for ideas.

2. Brush jam (strawberry, raspberry, orange marmalade or apricot) over a baked and cooled tart shell. Spoon the filling into the tart and drizzle with melted chocolate. Sprinkle with chopped nuts. Garnish with a big sprig of fresh mint.

Three Glazes for Fruit Tart

THE LIGHT COLORED GLAZE

Most glazes are made from jams and liquors. We will use all fruit jam (no sugar) and lemon juice.

GETTING STARTED
Small pot

INGREDIENTS
1/2 cup apricot or peach jam or orange marmalade
2 teaspoons to 1 tablespoon of lemon juice
1 tablespoon orange juice

1. Melt jam in small pot over low heat. Remove from heat and stir in lemon and orange juice. Push the glaze through a small strainer or use it, as I do, right out of the pot. If the glaze is too thick, add water.

2. Brush glaze onto fruit with small clean pastry brush.

THE RED GLAZE

Use a red jam (raspberry or strawberry) and follow the method described for making Light Colored Glaze.
If you cannot find seedless jam, you may want to press the glaze through a fine mesh strainer to eliminate the seeds.

THE RICE SYRUP GLAZE

A neutral taste and color is achieved with a rice syrup glaze.

Thin some rice syrup with a little water and brush it on a baked crust for great shine and taste.

Especially Good Fruit Combos For Tarts are,
Mango and Blackberry
Peach and Raspberry
Banana and Kiwi
Fresh Fig and Any Berry
Lemon Cream and Any Berry
Strawberry, Raspberry and Blueberry – A 4th of July Tart

 RUSTIC 3 BERRY PIE

9 TO 10-INCH FREEFORM GALETTE

Feel free to vary the fruit but maintain the 6 cup formula. If the oven is accurate, the pie will bake in 35 to 40 minutes. Longer baking causes the berries to burst—the juice will be lost.

GETTING STARTED

> One recipe Foolproof Flaky Pie Dough
> Preheated 425 degree oven
> Parchment paper for rolling dough
> Rolling pin
> Parchment-lined baking sheet
> Cooling rack

INGREDIENTS

> 1/2 cup maple sugar, divided (more to taste)
> 1/2 cup arrowroot, divided
> 1/4 teaspoon grated nutmeg or mace
> 1/4 teaspoon sea salt
> 2 cups strawberries, washed, hulled, halved if large
> 2 cups blueberries, washed and dried
> 2 cup raspberries, washed and dried (oh so gently)
> Optional: 1/3 cup berry, orange or apricot jam, warmed

1. Mix 1/4 cup maple sugar, 1/4 cup arrowroot, nutmeg and salt in a large bowl, stir in berries, reserving a few of each type. Set berries aside at room temperature for 20 minutes.

2. Remove pie dough from the refrigerator. Roll dough between 2 pieces of parchment paper into a large oval, about 12 inches. Slip a baking sheet under the parchment paper, cover the dough with plastic wrap and refrigerate again for at least 30 minutes.

3. Stir together the remaining 1/4 cup maple sugar and 1/4 cup arrowroot in a small bowl. Remove the dough from the refrigerator, unwrap and discard the plastic wrap. Sprinkle the maple-arrowroot combination over the center of the dough, leaving a 3-inch rim uncovered. Spoon the berries over the arrowroot–sugar mixture. (If the berries have released more than a few tablespoons of juice, leave some juice in the bowl). Fold dough up and over the filling. Bake the tart on a parchment lined baking sheet in the lower third of the oven for 35 to 45 minutes or until the pastry is lightly browned and the filling is bubbling.

4. Cool the pie on a rack. Do not slice until the pie has cooled at least 30 minutes; the juices need time to thicken.

GOOD BAKER'S TIPS & VARIATIONS

Berry pies do bubble over, but parchment keeps the mess off the floor of the oven. However, should you find your oven smoking for just that reason, throw salt on the spillover; it smothers the smoke. By the way, this is the one of the only uses for table salt.

BERRIED TREASURES

Blueberries, Blackberries, Strawberries, Raspberries, Huckleberries Sweet berries & Tart berries.

It is easy to get several servings of fruit into a daily meal plan.
Think about a beautifully arranged breakfast fruit salad, fruit on hot or cold cereal and fruit in smoothies. Make a smoothie by blending soy or ricemilk with fruit, healthy and satisfying. Use frozen fruit to make a thick, icy drink.

Most of us know that fruits and veggies taste best when they are in season.
Have you ever bitten into a big strawberry for instance, and wondered where the taste had gone. Today, berries are bred to hold up during long distance shipping and this has effectively ruined the taste of strawberries and other fruit.

Berries are nutrient-dense foods, low-calorie, fat-free and are naturally delicious simply eaten out of hand. Did you know that 1/2 cup of strawberries contains 40 mg of Vitamin C plus a good amount of fiber? All-American blueberries are low in calories, about 80 per cup and supply a respectable amount of potassium, fiber and vitamin C.

Select plump, fresh berries and as soon you return home check the berries, discarding any that are soft or moldy. One bad berry can ruin the whole batch.

Plan to use berries within a day or two and do not wash them until just before using and then very gently. Keep the green stems on strawberries until after they've been washed so they don't absorb water. Freeze extra berries in a single layer on a flat pan, then pour them into containers. Frozen berries (bananas too) added to non-dairy milks make delicious, healthful smoothies.

 Berry Crisp in a Cookie Piecrust

8 OR MORE SERVINGS

Have your pie and eat a crisp too. This recipe presents the technique for making a pressed crust; here it is wheat-free. Alternatively, lose the bottom crust and make a crisp. Or fill a baked crust with tofu cream and fruit, chocolate frosting and sorbet and so on. Both the filling and crust can be made ahead.

GETTING STARTED
    Preheated 375 degree oven
    Oiled 8-inch tart pan with removable bottom
    Cooling rack

INGREDIENTS: CRUST
    1 cup rolled oats, toasted and cooled
    1 cup nuts, toasted and cooled
    1/4 teaspoon sea salt
    1/2 teaspoon ground cinnamon
    1/4 cup oat, barley or spelt flour
    1/2 teaspoon baking powder
    3 tablespoons unsweetened dry coconut
    2 tablespoons canola oil
    3 tablespoons maple syrup
    1 to 3 tablespoons fruit juice or water
    2 teaspoons vanilla extract
    1/2 teaspoon almond extract

1. Grind oats, nuts, salt and cinnamon in the bowl of a food processor until very fine. Add flour and baking powder and pulse 2 to 3 times. Remove dry ingredients to a medium bowl and stir in coconut.

2. Mix oil, maple syrup and extracts in a small bowl until emulsified and add to dry ingredients. Mix until dough holds together when pinched. Add water slowly. If dough is too dry (crumbly), add juice or water, a tablespoon or less at a time. Turn dough out of bowl onto a large piece of plastic wrap and squeeze and press into a disk. Wrap tightly and chill 15 to 30 minutes. Bring dough to room temperature before pressing it into tart pan.

3. Press the dough evenly into the pan; plastic wrap on the dough is helpful. Be sure to make right angles where sides and bottom of pan meet or the dough will be too thick. Refrigerate crust for 30 minutes.

4. BAKE CRUST: Place the tart pan on a baking sheet and bake 15 to 18 minutes until golden brown. The crust will firm as it cools but is fragile when hot. Keep the crust in the pan until the tart is served. (continued, page 109)

BERRY CRISP IN A COOKIE PIECRUST

CONTINUED

INGREDIENTS: FILLING
> 3 cups blueberries, washed and patted dry
> 1/3 cup orange juice
> 1/4 cup all fruit jam plus 2 tablespoons for crust
> 2 teaspoons kuzu or 4 teaspoons arrowroot, dissolved in 1 tablespoon water
> 1 cup sliced strawberries
> 1 to 1 1/2 cups granola
> Optional: additional berries

1. Simmer blueberries with orange juice and 1/4 cup jam in a large skillet for 5 to 7 minutes, stirring a few times until the fruit is very hot. Add dissolved kuzu or arrowroot to berries, stirring constantly. Cook kuzu for 1 to 2 minutes after the boil, arrowroot only to the boil. Pour filling into a shallow bowl, cool and refrigerate.

ASSEMBLE THE CRISP

Spread the cooled crust with 2 tablespoons of all fruit jam. Drain the blueberries, reserving the juice. Spoon blueberries into the crust and top with the sliced strawberries. Pat granola onto the filling. Gently pull a few strawberries up to peek through the granola. Refrigerate the tart, in its pan, for at least 1 hour and up to 6 hours. Remove sides of pan just before serving. The reserved berry juice is delicious served as is, or with additional fruit added to it.

CHOCOLATE GLAZED STRAWBERRY SHORTCAKES

8 SHORTCAKES

Shortcakes are synonymous with summer and these might be the best. Tender chocolate-glazed, not too sweet biscuits are spread with jam, and piled high with cream and berries. The individual components of this recipe can be used in other ways. The biscuits are super simply spread with jam, and the strawberry sauce is terrific spooned over a slice of plain cake.

GETTING STARTED

Preheated 425 degree oven
Food processor
Parchment lined baking sheet
Cooling rack
1/4 cup Ultimate Chocolate Glaze (page78)

INGREDIENTS BERRY CREAM (2 CUPS)

1 pound firm silken tofu, steamed
3/4 cup all fruit berry jam plus 1/4 to 1/3 cup additional for spreading on biscuits
2 tablespoons lemon juice
1/3 cup maple sugar
1/2 teaspoon sea salt
1 tablespoon grated lemon zest
1 tablespoon vanilla extract
1 teaspoon lemon extract

1. Cream tofu in a food processor for about 3 to 4 minutes stopping to scrape down the sides twice. Add 1/2 cup jam, lemon juice, maple sugar, salt, zest and extracts. Continue to process until cream is very smooth. Refrigerate cream in a covered container at least 1 hour and up to overnight to allow flavors to blend.

FRESH STRAWBERRY SAUCE (2 CUPS)

The berries are not cooked; rather they are glazed with warm jam. Use this method to glaze other fruit, raspberries and blueberries for example.

INGREDIENTS

1/4 cup all fruit strawberry or seedless raspberry jam
2 tablespoons apple juice mixed with 2 teaspoons lemon juice
    or 2 tablespoons Cassis (a liqueur)
2 cups strawberries, sliced

1. Simmer jam and fruit juice or liqueur in a small pot over low heat until jam is melted, about 5 minutes. Stir berries into the hot sauce to coat and warm them but do not cook or the berries will turn gray. Serve Strawberry Sauce warm or at room temperature. (continued page 111)

INGREDIENTS SHORTCAKE BISCUITS

    2/3 cup whole wheat pastry flour
    1 1/3 cups unbleached white flour
    2 teaspoons baking powder
    1/2 teaspoon baking soda
    1/4 cup maple sugar
    1/4 teaspoon sea salt
    2/3 cup plus 1 tablespoon vanilla soymilk
    1 1/2 tablespoons canola oil
    1/2 teaspoon vanilla extract
    1/4 cup soymilk mixed with 2 tablespoons maple syrup
    2 to 4 tablespoons maple sugar for sprinkling
    1 3.5 ounce bar of dairy-free chocolate, melted

1. Sift dry ingredients into a medium bowl: flours, baking powder, baking soda, maple sugar and salt. Stir with a wire whisk to mix and aerate.

2. In another bowl, mix the wet ingredients until foamy: soymilk, oil and vanilla. Make a well in the center of the dry ingredients; pour the liquid in. Stir with a spoon only until a soft dough forms.

3. Turn dough out onto a lightly floured surface. Pat into a round about 1/2 inch thick. Cut dough into quarters with a floured knife, and then cut each quarter in half. Place biscuits onto the parchment lined baking sheet, brush tops lightly with sweetened soymilk and sprinkle with maple sugar. Put biscuits in the top third of oven, immediately lower the heat to 400 degrees and bake 8 to 10 minutes. Remove biscuits from baking sheet and cool 5 minutes on a wire rack. Wrap biscuits tightly; they become stale quickly.

ASSEMBLE THE SHORTCAKES

Use a serrated knife to cut the biscuits in half. Place the bottom half cut side up on a serving plate and spread with jam. Spoon tofu cream, glazed berries and any juice released by the berries over the biscuit. Top with biscuit "lid" spread with chocolate glaze and enjoy.

BLUEBERRY SLUMP

8 SERVINGS

Very low fat slumps, (only 1 1/2 tablespoons of oil in the whole recipe), cook on top of the stove and the biscuits actually steam. The recipe makes a cake-like slump. Any combination of berries and/or stone fruit makes a wonderful biscuit and fruit treat. The only problem here might be eating too much. Slumps are sometimes called grunts. The question is, do the biscuits slump into the fruit or do they grunt while they are steaming? Actually, slumps, grunts, cobblers and crisps are part of the same very old family that has been popular since colonial days.

GETTING STARTED
Pot or skillet with tight fitting lid, 8 to 10-inches in diameter at least 3- inches deep.

INGREDIENTS FILLING
2 2/3 cups blueberries, washed and patted dry

1/3 cup maple sugar or to taste

1/3 cup orange juice

2/3 cup water

INGREDIENTS BISCUITS
1 teaspoon apple cider vinegar

1/2 cup vanilla soymilk

1/2 cup whole wheat pastry

1/2 cup unbleached white flour

1/4 cup maple sugar

2 teaspoons baking powder

1 teaspoon baking soda

1/2 teaspoon cinnamon powder

1/4 teaspoon sea salt

1 tablespoon grated orange zest

1 1/2 tablespoons canola oil

1/2 teaspoon orange extract

1/2 teaspoon vanilla extract

MAKE THE FILLING
1. Put berries, maple sugar, juice and water into a pot, cover and cook over medium heat to a boil. Reduce heat and simmer fruit 3 to 4 minutes.

MAKE THE BISCUITS
1. Mix the vinegar and soymilk in a cup and set aside for 2 to 3 minutes. This is called clabbering and will result in a buttermilk substitute.

2. Sift dry ingredients into a medium bowl: flours, maple sugar, baking powder, baking soda, cinnamon and salt and stir with a wire whisk to mix. Stir in orange zest.

3. Add oil and extracts to clabbered soymilk and pour into the center of dry ingredients. Stir lightly with a spoon only until a soft batter forms. Drop batter, using a tablespoon, onto the hot fruit. Cover the pot tightly and cook over medium-low heat, without uncovering, about 25 minutes until biscuits look set and the fruit has cooked into a sauce.

4. Serve slump directly from the pot; the filling will be very juicy. After a few hours, the slump becomes more cake-like and equally delicious.

CRUMB TOPPING FOR COBBLERS & FRUIT PIES

3 CUPS

Also called streusel, this recipe can be prepared up to 3 days ahead.

GETTING STARTED
Medium bowl

INGREDIENTS
1 cup whole wheat pastry flour
1/2 cup unbleached white flour
1/2 cup maple sugar
1 cup coarsely chopped, toasted nuts
1/2 teaspoon sea salt
2 teaspoons cinnamon powder
1/4 to 1/3 cup canola oil
1 tablespoon vanilla extract
1 teaspoon almond extract
Optional: fruit juice as needed for moistening

1. Stir together all dry ingredients in a medium bowl: flours, maple sugar, nuts, salt and cinnamon. Mix oil with extracts and drizzle over dry ingredients. Mix to make big, fat crumbs. Pat crumb topping onto unbaked pies or cobblers and bake according to the particular recipe until the crumbs are golden brown.

GOOD BAKER'S TIPS & VARIATIONS
This recipe makes enough crumb (streusel) topping to cover a 9 to 10-inch pie.
Consider making a double recipe to keep in you freezer.

Baked Apple Biscuit Topped Cobbler

6 TO 8 SERVINGS

When sweet apples are used to make this cobbler, no additional sweetener is necessary. Taste and add sweetener when tart apples are used.

GETTING STARTED

Preheated 400 degree oven
2 quart baking dish
Parchment-lined baking sheet

INGREDIENTS: FILLING

1 1/2 pounds sweet apples, cored and sliced (7 to 8 cups)
1/2 cup raisins or other dried fruit
1 1/2 to 2 1/2 cups apple cider or juice
2 tablespoons lemon juice
1/4 teaspoon sea salt
1 teaspoon ground cinnamon
1/4 teaspoon ground nutmeg
1/4 teaspoon ground cloves
2 teaspoons kuzu or 4 teaspoons arrowroot, dissolved in 2 tablespoons water or juice

INGREDIENTS: TOPPING

3/4 cup vanilla soymilk
1 tablespoon lemon juice
1 cup unbleached white flour
1/4 cup plus 2 tablespoons whole wheat pastry flour
1/4 cup plus 2 tablespoons cornmeal
1/4 teaspoon sea salt

1 tablespoon baking powder
1/2 teaspoon baking soda
1/2 teaspoon cinnamon powder
1/4 cup canola oil
1/4 cup maple syrup
1 tablespoon vanilla extract

FILLING

1. Put sliced apples, raisins, juice, lemon juice, salt and spices into a medium pot. Cook over medium heat about 5 minutes, or until fruit is hot. Mix dissolved kuzu or arrowroot into the hot fruit. Cook kuzu for 2 to 3 minutes after the boil; arrowroot only to the boil. Keep filling warm while you prepare topping. Filling can be made 1 day in advance and gently warmed in the (covered) baking dish prior to adding the topping.

BISCUITS

1. Combine soymilk and lemon juice in a medium bowl and set aside 2 to 3 minutes to sour (clabber). This is "buttermilk."

2. Sift the dry ingredients: flours, cornmeal, salt, baking powder, baking soda and cinnamon into a medium bowl. Stir with a wire whisk to mix.

3. Mix oil, maple syrup and vanilla into the clabbered soymilk and pour over the dry ingredients. Stir with a spoon just until soft dough forms. Don't over mix.

4. Spread warm fruit into baking dish. Spoon the dough onto the fruit and bake 25 minutes until juices start bubbling. Reduce oven to 375 degrees and bake 10 minutes longer or until cobbler is lightly browned and the fruit juices look thickened. Cool the cobbler for 10 to 15 minutes before serving.

CREAMY STRAWBERRY & DATE FILLING

1 1/2 CUPS

Dried dates are decidedly sweet making no additional sweetener necessary. Use enough fruit to flavor and color the dates. This cream, based on a recipe taught in the Chef's Training Program at the Natural Gourmet Cookery School, in New York City, makes a good cake filling and base for a fruit tart. Use enough fresh fruit to color the filling which should taste of fresh fruit, not like a dried date eaten out of hand.

GETTING STARTED
Food processor

INGREDIENTS
1 cup soft, pitted dates
1 1/2 to 2 cups strawberries, cleaned
3 tablespoons all-fruit strawberry jam
1 teaspoon vanilla extract
2 to 4 teaspoons lemon or orange juice
1 teaspoon grated orange or lemon zest

1. Puree dates in a food processor, adding berries in batches until taste, color and texture are pleasing. Add extracts, juice and zest.

GOOD BAKER'S TIPS & VARIATIONS
5 ounces of pitted dates equals 1 cup
Replace dates with dried figs. Soften dried figs in orange juice then puree with the juice.
Replace dates with orange segments; add 1/2 teaspoon orange extract. Replace strawberry jam with orange marmalade, and increase zest to 2 teaspoons

Dates, like all dried fruits, should be stored tightly in a cool, dark place to protect against insect infestation.

It is contact with air, after uncooked fruits are dried, as well as enzymatic activity that causes the pulp to darken. The taste is not affected.

A sulfur dioxide solution is used to prevent darkening and retain moisture during the processing of conventionally dried fruits although the additive is known to cause mild to serious reactions in some individuals. The FDA, in 1986, banned the use of sulfites in fresh fruits and vegetables but has continued to allow its use in dried fruits, pickles and wine. Sulfite-free, naturally dried fruits are available. Darker and drier than the treated ones, the flavor of naturally dried fruit is superior.

HINT OF LEMON CUSTARD SAUCE

1 1/2 CUPS

Thickened, not thick, this almost pudding reminds me of a full-bodied Creme Anglaise (vanilla custard sauce). It is lovely spread onto a baked tart crust and piled thickly with berries and other summer fruit. Ricemilk is preferable to soymilk in this recipe, it makes a more delicate sauce, but soymilk can be used.

GETTING STARTED
Medium pot

INGREDIENTS
2 cups vanilla ricemilk
1 teaspoon agar flakes
1/4 cup maple sugar
2 1/2 tablespoons kuzu or 5 tablespoons arrowroot, dissolved in 1/3 cup natural lemonade
1 tablespoon lemon juice
1 teaspoon vanilla extract
1/2 teaspoon lemon extract
1 to 3 teaspoons grated lemon zest

1. Pour ricemilk into a small pot, sprinkle agar flakes on the liquid and allow agar to soften 10 minutes. Add maple sugar to the pot and over low heat, simmer agar until it is dissolved.

2. Add dissolved kuzu or arrowroot to the hot liquid, stirring constantly. The mixture will thicken immediately. Cook kuzu about 30 seconds, after the boil; arrowroot only until the boil. Remove the pot from the stove; add lemon juice, extracts and optional zest. Pour the custard sauce into a shallow bowl and refrigerate until it thickens, about 30 minutes.

3. The custard may be "gloppy." In that case, stir it vigorously with a fork and it will smooth out.

NOTES

Chapter 6

Serendipity

where do these recipes belong?

in your book, of course!

More Healthy Desserts 101
Enjoy!

ANNEMARIE'S APPLE JUICE KUZU PUDDING

1 SERVING

This is a sleeping pill, anti-anxiety medicine and simply a delicious pudding, really. I learned about kuzu, and how to make this pudding, when I was a student in Annemarie Colbin's popular Food and Healing class. The ideas and ingredients were new to me, sometimes even odd, but I tried them and liked them. This recipe has been published in so many books and magazines; it is hard to keep track. This recipe is found in Ms. Colbin's book, Food and Healing. Thank you, Annemarie.

GETTING STARTED
　　Small pot

INGREDIENTS
　　1 cup apple juice
　　1 tablespoon kuzu dissolved in 2 tablespoons water
　　1/2 teaspoon vanilla extract

1.　Heat the apple juice to a low boil, add dissolved kuzu stirring constantly and cook over medium heat for 1 to 2 minutes. The mixture, which is thick, is cloudy at first, but it will clear.

2.　Pour the pudding into a cup and enjoy it warm.

GOOD BAKER'S TIPS & VARIATIONS
Kuzu is used in this recipe specifically for its medicinal properties. It is a relaxant and digestive aid. You don't have to be 'Sleepless in Seattle' or any other town, to enjoy a good tasting pudding.

The Recipes

ANNEMARIE'S APPLE JUICE KUZU PUDDING

HOT COCOA

NEW YORK EGGLESS CREAM

INSTANT AMAZAKE N'ICE CREAM

SUPER STUFFED BAKED APPLES

VANILLA BEAN N'ICE MILK

ANYTIME MEUSLI

NUTTY FROZEN BANANA POPS

POACHED PEACHES (NECTARINES TOO)

OT COCOA

1 SERVING

Here is a full-bodied, low fat cocoa drink. Multiply the recipe by the number of servings you are preparing.

GETTING STARTED
Medium pot (with heavy bottom)
Ultimate Chocolate Sauce (page 78)

INGREDIENTS
1/4 cup Ultimate Chocolate Sauce, or to taste
1 cup soymilk or ricemilk
1/2 teaspoon vanilla extract

1. Heat the chocolate sauce with half the soymilk or ricemilk in a small pot over low heat, stirring until mixture is smooth. Add remaining non-dairy milk and simmer until hot. Remove from stove, stir in vanilla, pour into a cup and relax.

EW YORK EGGLESS CREAM

Those of you who remember egg creams probably have strong opinions about the brand of chocolate syrup, the order in which the ingredients are poured into the glass and mixed and the Brooklyn Dodgers. Let's not even go there. Try it, you'll like it. I developed this recipe several years ago for a recipe booklet distributed by Imagine Foods.

GETTING STARTED
Medium pot (with heavy bottom)
Ultimate Chocolate Sauce (page 78)

INGREDIENTS
1/4 cup Ultimate Chocolate Sauce, or to taste
1 cup vanilla soymilk or ricemilk
1/2 teaspoon vanilla extract
Fizzy water: seltzer, club soda or sparkling water.

1. Pour Ultimate Chocolate Sauce into a tall glass, mix in soy or rice milk and add fizzy water to taste.

 INSTANT AMAZAKE N'ICE CREAM

1 TO 2 SERVINGS

Amazake (ah-mah-ZAH-key) is a creamy, sweet beverage traditionally made by inoculating cooked rice with koji. (See Tips). Today, most amasake is made by substituting part or all of the koji with enzymes from sprouted grain grown specifically for this purpose. This type of amazake, high in glucose and maltose, makes a nourishing, low-fat, high-carbohydrate snack. In other words, amazake supplies quick energy. Different brands vary in consistency and taste. The amazake made by Grainaissance is available in many flavors and widely available. I intended to name this recipe amazake sorbet, but it really tastes more like dairy ice cream.

GETTING STARTED
Food processor
Frozen fruit, any

INGREDIENTS
8 ounces of amazake, any flavor
1 teaspoon vanilla extract
1/2 small frozen banana or 1/3 cup other frozen fruit

1. Freeze amazake in ice cube trays or a shallow container.

2. Process frozen amazake and vanilla in a food processor. Pulse several times until the amazake starts to break up, then process 1 to 2 minutes longer. Expect to see little pebbles, the amazake does not become smooth.

3. Cut frozen fruit into small piece, and add to the food processor. Process until fruit and amazake are blended. Serve as you would any frozen dessert.

GOOD BAKER'S TIPS & VARIATIONS
Koji is rice that has been inoculated with Aspergillus orzae. The koji reacts with the starch in the grain, making it sweet and highly digestible. This is an example of a food transformed, in this case, into a natural sweetener, without the use of chemicals or high tech processing.

While frozen amazake does not look smooth when processed it tastes creamy and quite rich, even without the addition of fruit.

Super Stuffed Baked Apples

6 TO 8 SERVINGS

Now here is a jazzy breakfast idea; top a warm baked apple with frozen vanilla soymilk and have dessert for breakfast. It looks legal to me.

GETTING STARTED
> Preheated 350 degree oven
> Apple Corer
> Shallow baking dish

INGREDIENTS
> 4 medium apples
> 1 1/2 to 2 cups apple juice
> 1/4 cup sulfite-free currants or raisins
> 3 tablespoons roasted, chopped nuts
> 1/2 teaspoon cinnamon powder
> 1/4 teaspoon mace or nutmeg
> 1/3 cup apple butter or any all-fruit jam

1. Core the apples from the top, stopping 1 inch from the bottom, and then peel the top 1/4 section of each apple. Put the apples into a shallow baking dish large enough so that the apples do not touch. Pour apple juice over the apples.

2. Mix the currants, nuts, cinnamon and mace or nutmeg in a small bowl. Spoon the fruit into the cavity of the apples; scatter leftover filling over the bottom of the baking dish. Cover the baking dish with parchment paper and over wrap with foil. Bake the apples for 25 minutes, uncover and baste the apples with pan juices. Bake 5 to 10 minutes longer, or until apples are tender but not mushy. The baking time depends upon the variety of apple used. Brush the apples with apple butter or jam, stirring any leftover into the pan juices.

3. Serve baked apples in individual bowls with warm pan juices.

Vanilla Bean n'ice Milk

3 CUPS

Good tasting non dairy frozen desserts are available in markets, but suppose it is late, all the shops are closed and you just need to have a spoonful or two of a frozen treat. Vanilla Bean N'Ice Milk comes to the rescue. Skip the freezing step and you have made creamy vanilla pudding.

GETTING STARTED
Medium pot

INGREDIENTS
2 cups vanilla soymilk
1/2 cup maple sugar
1 vanilla bean
2 tablespoons kuzu or 1/4 cup arrowroot, dissolved in 1/2 cup water
1 tablespoon vanilla extract

1. Mix maple sugar into soymilk. Cut vanilla bean lengthwise and scrape the seeds into the sweetened soymilk. Add the split bean and stir. Set aside to steep for 30 minutes.

2. Remove the vanilla bean, rinse, dry and save for another use. Heat the dissolved kuzu or arrowroot slowly over low heat in a pot with a heavy bottom, stirring with a wire whisk until the mixture is hot. Stir in 1 cup of soymilk. Keep the heat low and cook to just under a boil. Add the second cup of soymilk, stirring constantly until a gentle boil is reached. Be careful the bottom of the mixture does not scorch. Cook kuzu 1 to 2 minutes after a (low) boil and only to the boil when using arrowroot. Remove the pot from the stove and stir in vanilla extract.

3. Pour ice milk into a shallow container or individual ice cube trays and cool completely. Cover and place in the freezer until ice milk is solid. Before serving, soften Vanilla Bean N'Ice Milk: spoon it into a food processor and pulse the machine on and off a few times.

ANYTIME MUESLI

6 TO 8 SERVINGS

Muesli is also known as Swiss oatmeal and was invented by a Swiss physician for his patients. It is easy to digest and packed with iron, calcium, zinc and other important nutrients. This meusli is simply uncooked oatmeal, softened in liquid, juice or (non-dairy) milk and mixed with fruit, seeds and nuts. Vary the fruits and the amounts, according to your appetite and the season. Meusli topped with fresh fruit and soy yogurt is one of my favorite light suppers.

GETTING STARTED
    A bowl
    A knife or scissors for cutting dried fruit

INGREDIENTS
    1/2 cup rolled oats, toasted and cooled
    1/2 cup fruit juice or soy or ricemilk, more for serving
    2 tablespoons toasted sesame seeds
    2 tablespoons toasted sunflower seeds
    2 tablespoons toasted, chopped nuts
    2 tablespoons any sulfite-free dried fruit, (raisins, apricots, dates, apples)
    1 cup fresh fruit, (diced apple, pear, peach, berries)
    soy yogurt to taste

1. Mix oats and juice in a small bowl, cover and refrigerate overnight.

2. Just before serving, mix in all other ingredients and add soymilk, ricemilk or soy yogurt to taste.

GOOD BAKER'S TIPS & VARIATIONS
An overnight soak produces creamy muesli. I sometimes prefer more texture and soak the muesli for only 1 hour.

 Nutty Frozen Banana Pops

8 SERVINGS

I like these pops so much that I buy extra bananas to keep in the freezer. Frozen bananas are famous for tasting like ice cream. Most people do not know that grapes are fabulous frozen too; eating a frozen grape is like eating a bite of sorbet.

GETTING STARTED
Sheet pan lined with parchment paper
Pop-sticks (see note)

INGREDIENTS
4 large ripe bananas or 8 small ones
8 ounces dairy-free, refined sugar free chocolate or carob, chips or bar
1/2 cup chopped nuts or crushed granola, cookie crumbs or dried unsweetened coconut

1. Peel the bananas and cut each in half horizontally. Insert a wooden pop stick into each one. Place the bananas on the sheet pan, cover the pan and freeze the bananas for 4 hours to overnight.

2. When you are ready to assemble the bananas, melt the chocolate or carob a small, heatproof bowl set over simmering waterr; stir until melted. Scrape the chocolate or carob into a shallow dish; cool 5 minutes.

3. Spread chopped nuts, coconut, cookie crumbs or a combination, into a shallow bowl. This is the topping.

4. Assemble the pops: Dip a banana into the melted chocolate to coat. Let the excess chocolate drip back into the dish. Immediately roll the banana in the topping to coat. Repeat until all the bananas are coated. Place bananas on the lined sheet pan.; cover and freeze. They will be frozen in about 2 hours. The bananas can be made ahead and frozen for up to 2 weeks, tightly covered.

GOOD BAKER'S TIPS & VARIATIONS
If using bar chocolate or carob, break it into pieces before melting it.
Note: If you do not have pop-sticks, cut the bananas into bite size chunks, dip and coat, using a fork to spear or otherwise help you handle the bananas. Freeze and serve in cake cups.
Be sure to purchase carob chips made without hydrogenated or tropical oils; sometimes listed as fractionated oils. Carob chips sometimes contain dairy. Choose carefully.

 POACHED PEACHES (NECTARINES TOO)

4 SERVINGS

Elegant and easy poached fruit is naturally fat-free, sugar-free, cholesterol-free and tastes just great. Poaching fruit enhances its flavor. Even under ripe fruit poaches to a succulent sweetness. Orange Ginger Crisps (page 53) are a particularly good accompaniment to the poached peaches. Think about using different textures when designing a dessert, for example, crisp and creamy, crunchy and smooth.

GETTING STARTED
Medium pot with cover

INGREDIENTS
2 cups sugar free peach juice or natural lemonade
2 strips lemon zest
4 ripe peaches, washed

1. Put juice and lemon zest into a medium saucepan and bring to a low boil. Cook for 10 minutes. Put the peaches into the juice, reduce heat and simmer 10 minutes.

2. Use a slotted spoon to remove peaches from juice (which is now poaching liquid). Peel the peaches over a small bowl using a paring knife; the skin should slip off easily. Cut each peach in half and remove the pit, put peach halves into a bowl and set aside.

3. Bring the poaching liquid to a slow boil. Cook 15 to 20 minutes to reduce liquid. Pour hot juice over peaches. Cool and refrigerate. Serve peaches with the poaching liquid, plain or with a cream or fruit sauce.

GOOD BAKER'S TIPS & VARIATIONS
I suggest peeling the peaches over a bowl as a way to save any juice that may drip from the fruit.

NOTES

NOTES

NOTES

BIBLIOGRAPHY AND RECOMMENDED READING LIST

Barnard, Neal. *Eat Right Live Longer*. New York: Crown Trade Publishers, 1995.

Bergeron, Ken. *Professional Vegetarian Cooking*. New York: John Wiley & Sons, 1999.

Berley, Peter. *The Modern Vegetarian Kitchen*. New York: HarperCollins Publishers, 2000.

Bradford, Peter and Montse. *Cooking with Sea Vegetables*. Vermont: Healing Arts Press, 1985.

Braker, Flo. *The Simple Art of Perfect Baking*. New York: William Morrow and Company, Inc., 1885.

Carlson, Rachel. *Silent Spring*. Boston: Houghton, Mifflin, 1962 and 1987.

Clark, Robert. *Our Sustainable Table Essays*. California: North Point Press, 1990.

Coe, Sophie D. and Michael D. Coe. *The True History of Chocolate*. London: Thames and Hudson, Ltd. 1996.

Colbin, Annemarie. *Food and Our Bones*. New York: Plume, 1998.
        Food and Healing. New York: Ballantine Books, 1986.

Corriher, Shirley O. *CookWise*. New York: William Morrow and Company, 1997.

Davis, Gail. *The Complete Guide to Vegetarian Convenience Foods*. Oregon: Newsage, 1999.

Deibel, Karen. *Creating Peaceful Meals*. Ohio: Karen Deibel, 1998.

Dufty, William. *Sugar Blues*. New York: Warner Books, 1975.

Edwards, Linda. *Baking For Health*. New York: Avery Publishing Group Inc., 1998.

Eisman, George R.D. *The Most Noble Diet: Food Selection and Ethics*. New York: Diet Ethics, 1994.

Erasmus, Udo. *Fats and Oils*. Canada: Alive Books, 1986.

Gisslen, Wayne. *Professional Baking*. New York: John Wiley & Sons, Inc., 1985.

Grogan, Bryanna Clark. *Nonna's Italian Kitchen*. Tennessee: Book Publishing Company, 1998.
        The Almost No Fat Cookbook. Tennessee: Book Publishing Company, 1994.

Hagler, Louise. *Tofu Cookery*. Tennessee: Book Publishing Company, 1994.

Klaper, Michael. *Vegan Nutrition: Pure and Simple*. Hawaii: Gentle World, 1987.

Lappe, Frances Moore. *Diet for a Small Planet*. New York: Ballantine Books, 1971.

Madison, Deborah. *Vegetarian Cooking for Everyone*. New York: Broadway Books, 1997

Melina, Vesanto R.D., Davis, Brenda R.D. Harrison, Victoria R.D.,. *Becoming Vegetarian*.
                                        Tennessee: Book Publishing Company, 1995.

Messina, Mark Ph.D., Virgina Messina R.D. *The Simple Soybean and Your Health*.
                                        New York: Avery Publishing Group, 1994.

Ornish, Dean. *Dr. Dean Ornish's Program for Reversing Heart Disease*. Ballantine Books: New York, 1990.

Raymond, Jennifer. *The Peaceful Palate*. California: Heart and Soul Publications, 1992.

Robbins, John. *Diet For a New America*. New Hampshire: Stillpoint, 1987.

Root, Waverly. *Food*. New York: Simon and Schuster, 1980.

Sass, Lorna J. *Recipes from an Ecological Kitchen*. New York: William Morrow and Company, 1992.
        Shortcut Vegetarian. New York: Quill, 1997

Sax, Richard. *Classic Home Desserts*. Vermont: Chapters, 1994.

Stepaniak, Joanne. *Table For Two*. Tennessee: The Book Publishing Company, 1996.

Walters, Carole. *Great Pies and Tarts*. New York: Clarkson Potter Publishers. 1998.

Weill, Andrew MD. *8 Weeks to Optimum Health*. New York. Alfred A. Knopf, 1997.

Wittenberg, Margaret M. *Good Food: The Complete Guide to Eating Well*. California: The Crossing Press, 1995.

Your local Yellow Pages telephone book is a good place to look for ingredients and supplies. Check the listings for health, natural foods, Asian markets, baking supply, cake decorating and restaurant supply. Farmers markets and food cooperatives offer good quality and selection at reasonable cost. The following is a selected list of companies that provide good quality ingredients and supplies. There are many others.

CHOCOLATE AND SWEETENERS

AH!LASKA
distributed by Cool Fruits
941-561-3331
Cocoa powder and mixes

DAGOBA
Organic Chocolate
PO Box 2374 Boulder CO 80306
303-473-9632
www.dagobachocolate.com

GREEN & BLACK
Dairy-free organic, fair traded
Chocolate and cocoa powder
Distributed by Belgravia Imports
662 Bellevue Avenue, Newport, RI 02840
401-849-1122
www.demon.co.uk/EarthNet/gbs.home.

NEWMANS OWN ORGANICS
Organic Chocolates
Some are dairy-free
PO Box 2098, Aptos, CA 95001
408-685-2866S

RAPUNZEL™ ORGANIC CHOCOLATE
AND COCOA POWDER
800-297-2814

NSPIREDNATURAL FOODS
Formerly known as Sunspire
Grain and organic cane sweetened chocolates
510-568-0116
   includes
TROPICAL SOURCE CHOCOLATES
Kosher chocolate chips
Cloud Nine, Inc.

HIGHLANDS SUGARWORKS
PO Box 58 Pitman Road
Websterville VT 05678
802-479-1747
Grade B Maple Syrup, Mail order

SUZANNES SPECIALTIES
800-762-2135
morano@ifu.net
New Jersey
Brown Rice syrup and other sweeteners

VERMONT COUNTRY NATURALS
P.O. Box 240
 Charlotte, VT 05445
800-528-7021
Maple Syrup, Granulated Maple

WESTBRAE NATURAL FOODS
1065 East Walnut Street
Carson, NC 90303
310-866-8200
Organic Rice Syrup Rice Syrup, Soymilk
PO Box 2860
Daytona Beach, FL 32120
904-258-4708

WHOLESOME FOODS
Succanat (Su-gar Ca-ne Na-tural)
PO Box 2860
Daytona Beach, FL 32120
904-258-4708
Evaporated cane juice.
Organic available

MANUFACTURERS OF NATURAL FOODS

The following companies provide high-quality natural foods ingredients.

ARROWHEAD MILLS, INC.
Flours and other good quality
baking ingredients
PO Box 2059
Hereford, TX 79045
806-364-0730

BOB'S RED MILL NATURAL FOODS
Stone ground flours, much more
Some organic
5209 SE International Way
Milwaukee, OR 97222
503-654-3215
www.bobsredmill.com

COOK FLAVORING CO.
P.O. Box 890
Tacoma WA 98401
206-627-5499
Natural extracts

DIAMOND ORGANICS
Freedom, CA 95019
800-922-2396
Ships fresh organic produce
over night, the prices are
surprisingly affordable.

EDEN FOODS
Soymilk, ricemilk, oils, apple cider vinegar,
rice syrup, barley malt,
Agar flakes, bars and kuzu
701 Tecumseh Road
Clinton, Michigan 49236
800-248-0301/ www.edenfoods.com.

FRONTIER COOPERATIVE HERBS
Box 299, Norway, IA 52318
800-669-3275
Non-irradiated spices, organic vanilla and
other extracts

GRAINAISSANCE, INC.
1580 Emeryville, CA 94608
510-547-7256
Amazake rice beverage

GREAT EASTERN SUN
92 McIntosh Rd.
Asheville, NC 28806
800-334-5809
Sweet Cloud Brown Rice Syrup,
Organic

KING ARTHUR FLOUR
PO Box 1010
Norwich, VT 05055
802-649-3881
Flour and other baking supplies
The Baking Sheet newsletter
Organic flours, extracts
Mail order
www.kingarthurflour.com

SUZANNES SPECIALTIES
1 800-762-2135
MORANO@IFU.NET
Quality organic rice syrup and other
liquid sweeteners

IMAGINE FOODS
Specializes in products derived from rice,
Rice milk and frozen nondairy desserts
350 Cambridge Ave., Suite 350,
Palo Alto, CA 94306

MANUFACTURERS OF NATURAL FOODS

The following companies provide high-quality natural foods ingredients.

NASOYA FOODS, INC.
Excellent organic tofu
1 New England Way
Ayer, MA 01432
800-229-TOFU

OMEGA NUTRITION USA INC.
6515 Aldrich Rd.
Bellingham, WA 98226
800-661-3529
fresh pressed, unrefined oils
Organic unfiltered, unpasteurized
apple cider vinegar
www.omegaflo.com

PURITY FOODS, INC.
2871 W. Jolly Rd.
Okemos, MI 48864
800-999SPELT (spelt flour)

SPECTRUM NATURALS
Petaluma CA 94952A variety of oils
800-995-2705
www.spectrum naturals.com

WALNUT ACRES ORGANIC FARMS.
Extensive catalog of natural foods
Organic pumpkin puree.
Penns Creek, PA 17862
800-433-3993

VITASOY USA. INC.
PO Box 2012
S. San Francisco, CA 94083
800-VITASOY
Organic soymilks

MAIL ORDER CATALOGS FOR BAKING SUPPLIES AND EQUIPMENT ARE PLENTIFUL.

CUISINARTS
800-726-0190
Quality food processors

COOKING BY THE BOOK
212-966-9799
Remarkable new zester
13 Worth Street, NYC, NY 10013
www.cookingbythebook.com

KITCHENAID
800-253-1301
Quality food processor: with a large
and small bowl
Blenders

NEW YORK CAKE & BAKING DISTRIBUTORS
212-496-1234
56 West 22 Street NYC, NY 10010
212-675-2253 Catalog available

SUR LA TABLE
800-243-0852
Mail order and retail stores and catalog

WILLIAMS SONOMA
800-541-2233
PO Box 7456 - San Francisco, CA 94901
Mail order, catalog available

ZABARS
2245 Broadway, NYC, NY 10024
Mail order, catalog available

PUBLICATIONS & ORGANIZATIONS

A GOOD LIFE
A bimonthly magazine and wonderful read, this an excellent, information packed resource has something for everyone. Parents will find the information especially helpful.
Barbara McNally
245 Eighth Avenue Box 400, NYC, NY 10011

CENTER FOR SCIENCE IN THE PUBLIC INTEREST
Publishers of Nutrition Action Newsletter
Suite 300, 1875 Connecticut Avenue NW
Washington, DC 20009-5728

THE CHEFS COLLABORATIVE 2000
Associated with Oldways Trust (see listing) is a network of chefs who collectively and actively promotes sustainable food choice.

EARTHSAVE INTERNATIONAL
800- 362-3648
600 Distillery Commons
Louisville, KY 400206
www.earthsave.org/
This organization offers a great deal of good information from friendly staffers and volunteers.
John Robbins, the author of Diet for a New America, founded Earthsave.

NATURAL GOURMET COOKERY SCHOOL
48 West 21st Street, NYC, NY 10010
212-645-5170
www.naturalgourmetschool.com
A 600-hour professional chef training is offered several times a year. Full and part-time classes are available. The associated Natural Gourmet Institute for Food and Health offers a variety of cooking, baking and lecture classes to the public taught by Ms. Annemarie Colbin, the school's founder and many other instructors. Friday night dinners prepared by students in the professional program are very popular, reservations are suggested.

NORTH AMERICAN VEGETARIAN SOCIETY. (NAVS)
518-568-7970
P.O. Box 72, Dolgeville, NY 13329
518-568-7970
www.cyberveg.org/navs/
NAVS is a great resource for books and magazines and a subscription to its magazine, Vegetarian Voice, free with membership. The annual Summerfest held in July is fun and informative. Delicious vegan meals are served, supervised by Olympics gold medal winner and author, Ken Bergeron.

PUBLICATIONS & ORGANIZATIONS

OLDWAYS PRESERVATION & EXCHANGE TRUST
45 Milk Street, Boston, MA 021091
800-340-2300
Oldways is a non-profit educational organization dedicated to preserving healthy, environmentally sustainable food and agricultural traditions of many cultures.

PHYSICIANS COMMITTEE FOR RESPONSIBLE MEDICINE (PCRM)
PO Box 6322
Washinton, DC 20015
202-686-2210
www.sai.com/pcrm/
A non-profit organization of with made up of over 4000 physicians-members and lay-people who the choice of diet and believe diet and lifestyle affect health. PCRM focuses on preventative medicine and promotes vegan diet, ethical research methods and compassionate medical policy.

PURE FOOD CAMPAIGN
800-253-0681
The group supports an international ban on genetically engineered foods and reforming school food programs.

VEGETARIAN RESOURCE GROUP
PO Box 1463
Baltimore, MD 21203
410-366-VEGE
www.vrg.org
VRG promotes vegan and vegetarian nutrition. Vegetarian Journal is published bimonthly and is included with membership.

VEG NEWS
PO Box 2129
Santa Cruz, CA 95063-2129
408-358-6478
North America's monthly vegetarian newspaper

INDEX

To add your name to Fran's mailing list, request information about classes and to order copies of
GREAT GOOD DESSERTS NATURALLY send a note to:

FRAN COSTIGAN
For Gooodness Cakes
295 Greenwich Street PMB115 • NYC, NY 10007-1049
Vegiecake@aol.com

Chef-instructor Fran Costigan specializes in non-dairy, naturally sweetened organic desserts and health-supportive cuisine.

A graduate of the New York Restaurant School, Fran worked in "sugar-butter-cream" establishments until her interest in natural foods an vegetarian diet led her to the Natural Gourmet Cookery School. Her lively classes at the school continue to demonstrate the ease and joy of healthful diet. Dubbed a pioneering pastry chef, Fran has developed many courses at the school, including the Natural Pastry Arts Intensive.

Stints as pastry chef at NYC's Angelica Kitchen and Luma reinforced Fran's belief that the key to developing wonderfully textured, refined sugar-free dairy-free (vegan) desserts, was linking traditional pastry techniques to the unique properties of whole foods. This union was successful and a business born. Now brides and grandma's, artists and students rely on - Fran's For Goodness Cakes: The Chocolate Cake to Live For, 24 Karat Cake, Frankly Amazing Brownies, Chewy Oatmeal Raisin Cookies and more.

Fran's recipes and articles have been featured in publications including DELICIOUS! Magazine and Natural Health and she is a regular presenter at conferences throughout the country.

Professional affiliations include the International Association of Culinary Professionals, Women Chefs and Restaurateurs and Chef's Collaborative 2000.

Fran lives in New York City, New York.